Praise for
# THE WILLOUGHBYS

# THE WILLOUGHBYS

## by Lois Lowry

WITH ILLUSTRATIONS

BY THE AUTHOR

HOUGHTON MIFFLIN HARCOURT
BOSTON   NEW YORK

The Library of Congress has cataloged the hardcover edition as follows:
Lowry, Lois.
The Willoughbys / by Lois Lowry.
p. cm.
"Walter Lorraine books."
Summary: In this tongue-in-cheek take on classic themes in children's
literature, the four Willoughby children set about to become "deserving
orphans" after their neglectful parents embark on a treacherous around-
the-world adventure, leaving them in the care of an odious nanny.
[1. Orphans—Fiction. 2. Brothers and sisters—Fiction.
3. Family life—Fiction. 4. Humorous stories.] I. Title.
PZ7.L9673Wi 2008
[Fic]—dc22

ISBN: 978-0-618-97974-5 hardcover
ISBN: 978-0-358-42472-7 paper over board

Manufactured in the United States of America
DOC 10 9 8 7 6 5 4 3 2 1
4500795336

*für meine deutschen Mädchen,*
*Nadine und Annika*

# CONTENTS

# 1.

## THE OLD-FASHIONED FAMILY
## AND THE BEASTLY BABY

Once upon a time there was a family named Willoughby: an old-fashioned type of family, with four children.

The eldest was a boy named Timothy; he was twelve. Barnaby and Barnaby were ten-year-old twins. No one could tell them apart, and it was even more confusing because they had the same name; so they were known as Barnaby A and Barnaby B. Most people, including their parents, shortened this to A and B, and many were unaware that the twins even *had* names.

There was also a girl, a timid, pretty little thing with eyeglasses and bangs. She was the youngest, just six and a half, and her name was Jane.

They lived in a tall, thin house in an ordinary city and they did the kinds of things that children in old-fashioned stories do. They went to school and to the seashore. They had birthday parties. Occasionally they were taken to the circus or the zoo, although they did not care much for either, excepting the elephants.

Their father, an impatient and irascible man, went to work at a bank each day, carrying a briefcase and an umbrella even if it was not raining. Their mother, who was indolent and ill-tempered, did not go to work. Wearing a pearl necklace, she grudgingly prepared the meals. Once she read a book but found it distasteful because it contained adjectives. Occasionally she glanced at a magazine.

The Willoughby parents frequently forgot that they had children and became quite irritable when they were reminded of it.

Tim, the eldest, had a heart of gold, as many old-fashioned boys do, but he hid it behind a somewhat bossy exterior. It was Tim who decided what the children would do: what games they would play

("We'll have a game of chess now," he occasionally said, "and the rules are that only boys can play, and the girl will serve cookies each time a pawn is captured"); how they would behave in church ("Kneel nicely and keep a pleasant look on your face, but think only about elephants," he told them once); whether or not they would eat what their mother had cooked ("We do *not* like this," he might announce, and they would all put down their forks and refuse to open their mouths, even if they were very, very hungry).

Once, his sister whispered to him privately, after a dinner they had refused to eat, "I liked it."

But Tim glared at her and replied, "It was stuffed cabbage. You are not allowed to like stuffed cabbage."

"All right," Jane said with a sigh. She went to bed hungry and dreamed, as she often did, about becoming older and more self-assured so that someday she could play whatever game she liked or eat any food she chose.

Their lives proceeded in exactly the way lives proceeded in old-fashioned stories.

One day they even found a baby on their doorstep. This happens quite often in old-fashioned stories. The Bobbsey Twins, for example, found a baby on their doorstep once. But it had never happened to the Willoughbys before. The baby was in a wicker basket and wearing a pink sweater that had a note attached to it with a safety pin.

"I wonder why Father didn't notice it when he left for work," Barnaby A said, looking down at the basket, which was blocking the front steps to their house when the four children set out one morning to take a walk in the nearby park.

"Father is oblivious—you know that," Tim pointed out. "He steps over any obstructions. I expect he poked it aside." They all looked down at the basket and at the baby, which was sound asleep.

They pictured their father taking a high step over it after moving it slightly out of his way with his furled black umbrella.

"We could set it out for the trash collector," Barnaby B suggested. "If you take one handle, A, and I take the other, I believe we could get it down the stairs without much trouble. Are babies heavy?"

"Please, could we read the note?" asked Jane, trying to use the self-assured voice that she practiced in secret.

The note was folded over so that the writing could not be seen.

"I don't think it's necessary," Tim replied.

"I believe we should," Barnaby B said. "It could possibly say something important."

"Perhaps there is a reward for finding the baby," Barnaby A suggested. "Or it might be a ransom note."

"You dolt!" Tim said to him. "Ransom notes are sent by the ones who *have* the baby."

"Maybe we could send one, then," said Barnaby A.

"Perhaps it says the baby's name," said Jane. Jane was very interested in names because she had always felt she had an inadequate one, with too few syllables. "I would like to know its name."

The baby stirred and opened its eyes.

"I suppose the note might give instructions about babies," Tim said, peering down at it. "It might say where to put them if you find one."

The baby began to whimper and then very quickly the whimper changed to a yowl.

"Or," said Barnaby B, holding his ears, "how to keep them from screeching."

"If the note doesn't tell the name, may I name it?" Jane asked.

"What would you name it?" Barnaby A asked with interest.

Jane frowned. "Something with three syllables, I think," she said. "Babies deserve three syllables."

"Brittany?" Barnaby A asked.

"Possibly," Jane replied.

"Madonna?" Barnaby B suggested.

"No," Jane said. "Taffeta, I think."

By now the baby was waving its fists, kicking its chubby legs, and crying loudly. The Willoughbys' cat appeared at the front door, gazed briefly down at the basket, twitched its whiskers, and then dashed back inside as if it was made nervous by the sound. The baby *did* sound a bit like a yowling kitten; perhaps that was why.

Tim finally reached down past the flailing little fists and unpinned the note. He read it silently. "The usual," he said to the others. "Pathetic. Just what I expected."

He read it aloud to them. "'I chose this house because it looks as if a happy, loving family lives here, prosperous enough to feed another child. I am very poor, alas. I have fallen on hard times and cannot care for my dear baby. Please be good to her.'"

"Take that handle, twins," Tim said to his brothers. He took hold of the opposite handle. "Jane, you carry the note. We'll take the whole disgusting thing inside."

Jane took the folded note and followed behind her brothers, who picked up the basket, carried it into the front hall of the house, and set it there on an Oriental rug. The noise coming from the baby was not insignificant.

Their mother, frowning, opened the door at the end of the long hall. She emerged from the kitchen. "Whatever is that noise?" she asked. "I am trying to remember the ingredients for meat loaf and I cannot hear myself think."

"Oh, someone has left a beastly baby on our front steps," Tim told her.

"My goodness, we don't want a baby!" their mother said, coming forward to take a look. "I don't like the feel of this at all."

"I'd like to keep it," Jane said in a small voice. "I think it's cute."

"No, it's not cute," Barnaby A said, looking down at it.

"Not cute at all," Barnaby B agreed.

"It has curls," Jane pointed out.

Their mother peered at the baby and then reached toward the basket of beige knitting that she kept on a hall table. She removed a small pair of gold-plated scissors and snipped them open and closed several times, thoughtfully. Then she leaned over the basket and used the scissors.

"Now it doesn't have curls," she pointed out, and put the scissors away.

Jane stared at the baby. Suddenly it stopped crying and stared back at her with wide eyes. "Oh, dear. It isn't cute without curls," Jane said. "I guess I don't want it anymore."

"Take it someplace else, children," their mother said, turning back toward the kitchen. "Dispose of it. I'm busy with a meat loaf."

The four children lugged the basket back outside. They thought. They discussed the problem. It was Barnaby A, actually, who came up with a plan, which he explained to Tim, since he made all the decisions for the group.

"Fetch the wagon," Tim commanded.

The twins got their wagon from where it was kept, along with bicycles, under the stoop of the house. The boys set the basket inside the wagon while their sister watched. Then, taking turns pulling the handle of the wagon, they transported the baby in its basket down the block, across the street (waiting carefully for the light), and for two more blocks and around the corner to the west, going some distance farther until, reaching their destination, they finally stopped in front of a very forbidding house that was known as the Melanoff mansion. The gentleman who lived there was a millionaire. Maybe even a billionaire. But he never came out. He stayed  indoors, with the moldy curtains drawn, counting his money and feeling hostile. As with Scrooge from another old-fashioned story, tragic events in his past had caused him to lose interest in life.

The mansion was much larger than the other houses in the neighborhood, but it was unkempt. A wrought-iron fence around its yard was tilted and twisted in places, and the yard itself was cluttered with pieces of discarded furniture. Some of the windows were broken and boarded over, and a thin cat scratched itself and meowed on the porch.

"Wait, A," said Tim, when his brother began to push open the front gate. "I need to add to the note." He held his hand out to Jane, who had placed the folded paper carefully in the pocket of her ruffled frock, and she gave it to him.

"Pencil," Tim demanded, and one of the twins—for all the children were accustomed to carrying whatever Tim might need and demand—handed him a pencil.

Barnaby B turned so that Tim could use his back for a table.

"Could you tell what I wrote, B?" Tim asked his brother when he had finished.

"No. It felt like scribbles."

"You must train yourself better," Tim pointed out. "If *my* back had been the table, I would be able to recite each word and also the punctuation. Practice when you have a chance." Barnaby B nodded.

"You, too, A," Tim said, looking at the other twin.

"I will," Barnaby A promised.

"So will I," offered Jane.

"No. You needn't, because you are a girl. You will never be called upon for important work," Tim told her.

Jane began to cry a little, but very quietly, so that no one would notice. She vowed, through her quiet little tears, that one day she would prove Tim wrong.

"Here is what I wrote," Tim told them, holding up the note. He read it aloud. "'P.S. If there is any reward to be had for this beastly baby, it should go to the Willoughbys.'"

The other children nodded. They thought the P.S. was a good idea.

"You might say *must* instead of *should,*" Barnaby B proposed.

"Good idea, B. Turn around."

Barnaby B turned and Tim used his back for a table again, erasing one word and replacing it with the other, which Barnaby B could feel him underline. Then Tim read it aloud: "'If there is any reward to be had for this beastly baby, it *must* go to the Willoughbys.'"

He refolded the note and leaned down toward the basket. Then he paused.

"Turn again, B," he commanded. After his brother had turned to make a table of his back one more time, Tim wrote an additional sentence. He folded the note and pinned it to the baby's sweater.

"Get the gate, Jane," Tim said, and she pulled it open. "Now, one, two, three: HOIST!" Together the boys lifted the basket containing the baby from the wagon. They carried it to the sagging, dusty porch of the mansion and left it there.

The Willoughbys walked home.

"What did you add to the note at the end, Tim?" Barnaby A asked.

"Another P.S."

"What did it say, Tim?" asked Barnaby B.

"It said, 'Her name is Ruth.'"

Jane pouted. "Why?" she asked.

"Because," Tim said with a sly smile, "we are the ruthless Willoughbys."

# 2.
## A PARENTAL CONSPIRACY

Mr. and Mrs. Willoughby were seated in front of the fireplace after dinner. He was reading a newspaper, and she was knitting something out of beige wool.

The four children, in flannel pajamas, entered the room.

"I'm making the cat a sweater," Mrs. Willoughby told them, holding up the knitting, in which one small, thin sleeve had already been formed.

"I was hoping maybe you were making a second sweater for me and B," Barnaby A said. "It's difficult taking turns with a sweater."

"I've explained and explained," their mother said in

exasperation. "A, you wear it on Monday, Wednesday, and Friday. B, you have Tuesday, Thursday, Saturday. On Sunday you can fight over it."

She turned to her husband. "It's disgusting," she said, "the way children today all want their own sweaters." She knit a few more stitches industriously.

"Children?" Mr. Willoughby said in an impatient voice, putting his newspaper down. "Did you want something?"

"We were hoping that perhaps you would read us a story," Tim said. "Parents in books always read stories to their children at bedtime."

"I believe the mother usually does that," Mr. Willoughby said, looking toward his wife.

"I'm busy," Mrs. Willoughby said. "The cat needs a sweater." Hastily she knit another stitch.

Mr. Willoughby scowled. "Hand me a book," he said.

Tim went to the bookcase and began fingering the volumes that were lined on the shelf. "Make it fast," his father said. "I'm in the middle of an article about interest rates."

Quickly Tim handed him a volume of fairy tales. His father opened it in the middle as the children arranged themselves in a semicircle by his feet. They looked like a painting on a Christmas card. "God bless us, every one!" murmured Barnaby A, but Tim poked him. Mr. Willoughby began to read aloud.

> *Hard by a great forest dwelt a poor woodcutter with his wife and his two children. The boy was called Hansel and the girl Gretel. He had little to bite and to break, and once when great dearth fell on the land, he could no longer procure even daily bread. Now when he thought over this by night in his bed, and tossed about in his anxiety, he groaned and said to his wife: "What is to become of us? How are we to feed our poor children, when we no longer have anything even for ourselves?" "I'll tell you what, husband," answered the woman. "Early tomorrow morning we will take the children out into the forest to where it is the thickest; there we will light a fire for them, and give each of them one more piece of bread, and then we will go to our work and leave them alone. They will not find the way home again, and we shall be rid of them."*

Jane's lower lip trembled and she gave a small sob. Barnaby A and Barnaby B looked very nervous. Tim scowled.

"The end," said their father, closing the book with a snap. "Bedtime."

Silently, though Jane was still sniffling, the children scurried away and up the staircase to bed. Mrs. Willoughby turned to her needles and began a new row of stitches. Mr. Willoughby picked up his newspaper but did not begin reading again. Instead, he stared into space for a moment. Then he said, "Dearest?"

"Yes, dearest?"

"I need to ask you a question." He chewed his lip briefly.

"Yes, dearest?"

"Do you like our children?"

"Oh, no," Mrs. Willoughby said, using her gold-plated scissors to snip off a bit of yarn that had made a snarl. "I never have. Especially that tall one. What is his name again?"

"Timothy Anthony Malachy Willoughby."

"Yes, him. He's the one I least like. But the others are awful, too. The girl whines incessantly, and two days ago she tried to make me adopt a beastly infant."

Her husband shuddered.

"And then there are the two that I can't tell apart," Mrs. Willoughby went on. "The ones with the sweater."

"The twins."

"Yes, them. Why on earth do they look so much alike? It confuses people and isn't fair."

"I have a plan," Mr. Willoughby said, putting his paper down. He stroked one eyebrow in a satisfied way. "It's thoroughly despicable."

"Lovely," said his wife. "A plan for what?"

"To rid us of the children."

"Oh goodness, do we have to walk them into a dark forest? I don't have the right shoes for that."

"No, this is a better plan. More businesslike."

"Oooh, goody. I'm all ears," she replied with a malevolent smile, as she meticulously dropped a few stitches to make a hole for the cat's tail.

# 3.
## CONTEMPLATING
## ORPHANHOOD

"Shouldn't we be orphans?" Barnaby B asked.

The Willoughby children were seated on the front steps playing a complicated game to which only Tim knew the rules.

"Why?" asked Barnaby A, moving down a step because the rules said he must if he asked a question, and of course "Why?" was a question.

"Because," Barnaby B explained, "we are like children in an old-fashioned book. And—"

"Mostly they are orphans," Jane said. She moved down two steps because she had interrupted, which was against the rules, and now she was the lowest of the four.

"Worthy and deserving orphans," Barnaby B added.

"Winsome, too," added Jane.

The three younger children each moved down one more step just on general principles. Only Tim, who had invented the game and its rules, remained at the top of the short staircase that led to the front door. "I win," he announced. "Let's play one more time."

They all moved to sit side by side on the middle step.

"The baby we left at the mansion was an orphan," Jane pointed out, "but she wasn't deserving at all, or worthy or winsome."

"Don't be such a dodo, Jane," Tim said. "You have to move down a step for that. Ruth was not an orphan."

With a sigh, Jane moved down. "But—" she began.

"She had a mother, dodo. She had a hideous mother who abandoned her in a basket. A true orphan has a dead father and then perhaps a mother who dies of cholera in India, like Mary Lennox in *The Secret Garden*."

"Oh, yes!" said Jane, enthusiastically remembering. "Or Pollyanna! Her parents were dead so she got to take a long train ride all by herself! And Anne of Green Gables, remember? She came straight from the orphan asylum!

"Those are all girls, though," she added. "I wonder if there are boy orphans."

"Yes. James. The Giant Peach fellow. His parents were eaten by a hippo who escaped from the zoo," Barnaby B pointed out.

"Down one step, B," Tim commanded.

"Why?"

"For not saying *hippopotamus.* Willoughbys do not use silly nicknames."

"I think it was a rhino, actually," Barnaby A said, still thinking about James. "Oops. Sorry," he said when Tim glared. "I meant rhinoceros."

"But your full name is Timothy Anthony Malachy Willoughby." Barnaby B pointed out. "Isn't 'Tim' a silly nickname?"

Tim simply pointed to a lower step. Barnaby B moved down. His twin joined him.

"I do like the idea of us being orphans, though," Tim said. "I'll let you come up one step for thinking of it, B. And I'll move up one at the same time."

They shifted steps.

"I suppose we must do away with our parents somehow," Tim said. "I'm moving up for having that brilliant thought." He moved to the next-to-top step.

"I don't like them very much anyway," said

Barnaby B. "Mother makes us wear this bilious beige sweater. The sleeves are too long." He held up one arm and showed them. "I definitely don't like her. Father either."

"Nor do I," added Barnaby A. "Father is neglectful, and Mother is a vile cook."

"Jane?" Tim gave his sister a questioning look.

Jane shrugged. "I'm at the very bottom step," she said sadly. "I can't go any lower."

"We could put you in the coal bin in the basement," Tim pointed out, "and we will, if you say you are fond of our parents."

Jane thought. "No," she said. "I'm not. Not especially."

"Good answer," Tim announced. "I move to the top step for getting that good answer out of Jane."

He moved up. "I win," he said. "Again. You people don't *try*."

"May I speak?" Barnaby A asked from his low step. Tim nodded permission.

"A sea voyage sometimes produces orphans," Barnaby A pointed out. "There are often pirates. Or icebergs."

"And sea serpents," his twin added, "even though I don't entirely believe in sea serpents."

"I believe in giant squids," Jane said with a shudder.

"Good point," Tim acknowledged. "And piranhas. Are our parents planning a vacation, by any chance? On a ship?"

"I don't know."

"I don't know."

"I don't know."

The three younger children spoke at the same time and were each demoted one step for being monotonous and sounding like echoes, even though the game had ended.

"And now," Tim announced, going to retrieve his bicycle from under the stoop, "I am going out for a bit, to visit the Reprehensible Travel Agency and obtain some brochures. I have come up with a perfectly despicable plot to get rid of our parents."

"You *are* ruthless, Tim," Barnaby A commented happily.

"Yes. And soon to be an orphan, as well."

# 4.

## An Impending Vacation

"Dear ones," Mrs. Willoughby said at dinner as she sliced the overcooked leg of lamb with a small handsaw, "Father and I have decided to take a vacation."

"A sea voyage?" asked Tim, as he spooned some glutinous gravy onto the gray slab of meat she had given him.

"Why, yes," his mother replied. "As a matter of fact, we are taking a long sea voyage, with many interesting stops along the way. This very colorful brochure appeared through our mail slot, from the—let's see, what was that name again?" She picked up the glossy paper and looked at it.

"The Reprehensible Travel Agency?" suggested Tim.

"That's it exactly!" His mother beamed at him. "You're so clever, son. I hope your cleverness will win you a scholarship so that you can go to college."

"What about B and me?" Barnaby A asked. "We're not clever."

"And Jane? She's a complete dodo," Barnaby B added. "Does that mean that we won't be able to go to college?"

Their father glared at them. "You can read, can't you?" he asked.

"Yes, of course we can read," the twins replied.

"Even I can read," Jane said, "and I'm a complete dodo."

"Well, then, you should feel very fortunate. There are many less fortunate people in the world. I have heard of people in underdeveloped countries who do not know how to read.

"Here," he said, and he took the brochure from his wife and handed it to Barnaby B. "This is a test. Read this or you'll have no dessert."

Barnaby B looked with interest at the first glossy page of the brochure. "'Visit exotic locations,'" he read aloud.

"Now your brother," said Mr. Willoughby, and

grabbed the brochure. He handed it to Barnaby A, who read aloud: "'Erupting volcanoes. Ferocious wild animals. Floods, famine, and—'"

"And finally the girl." Mr. Willoughby grabbed the brochure again and handed it to Jane. She sounded out the words very carefully. "'Earthquakes. Civil strife. War zones.'"

"Good. You can all read. Dessert for everyone, and no college. You don't need college." Mr. Willoughby put his fork down. "Dearest?" He looked inquiringly at his wife. "Shall we tell them about our plans?"

"Please do," she said.

"We've decided, as a result of this glossy brochure from the Reprehensible Travel Agency, to take a vacation," Mr. Willoughby announced.

"Yes, you said that already," Jane pointed out.

"Don't interrupt."

"Sorry," said Jane, looking at her lap.

"Therefore," he continued, "since it is against the law for us to leave you alone—"

"It is?" asked Barnaby A with interest.

"We don't mind staying alone," Tim said. "We prefer it, actually."

Mr. Willoughby glared at the children. "May I continue?" he asked pointedly.

The children nodded politely. "Sorry," they all murmured, and Tim, feeling thwarted, kicked the cat under the table.

"Therefore," his father continued, "we have decided to hire a nanny."

## 5.

## THE ARRIVAL OF THE
## ODIOUS NANNY

"Here comes another one," Barnaby A announced, looking down from the window after the doorbell had sounded below.

The Willoughby children were on the fourth floor of the tall, thin house, the floor where a musty, cobwebbed attic had been converted into a musty, cobwebbed playroom.

"What does this one look like?" Barnaby B asked, glancing over from the table, where he was drawing a picture of a skyscraper on a long piece of paper that he had laid out. "Eighty-nine, ninety," he murmured as he drew two more windows. Barnaby B was meticulous, and he had decided that his skyscraper would have three hundred and thirty-six windows, twelve per floor, and that each one must be identical to the others. He measured them with a ruler, drew them with faint pencil lines, then went over each line with ink.

"Heavyset," his twin described, "and wearing a hat."

"I'm deducting four points from your daily total, A," Tim said, "because you did not include any helpful details." He put down his book, went to the window with a pair of binoculars, and looked down through them to the front steps. "Large feet wearing suede lace-up shoes," he announced, "a faux alligator purse, no gloves, a man's watch on the left wrist, the hat has a faded pink flower on its left side, and she is holding a torn piece of newspaper, probably the ad for a nanny."

Jane, who had been laboriously writing a note that she planned to pin to the sweater worn by an old doll, went to the window. "May I look?" she asked Tim.

"No," he said. "And a two-point deduction for

asking. Now she is about to ring the bell a second time. She has aimed her right index finger."

The bell sounded again.

"I get forty points for a correct prediction," Tim said.

"Do you think she looks villainous, like the one who came yesterday?" Barnaby B asked. "Ninety-two," he murmured, inking in another window.

"No. The one yesterday had some weaponry in her satchel," Tim said. "I was quite certain about that. No wonder Father ordered her to leave before he even interviewed her. Father dislikes weaponry of any sort."

"Yes, he's even suspicious of Mother's knitting scissors," Barnaby B pointed out. "He feels all warfare should be conducted with taunts and gibes and vicious rumors."

"What about the one the day before?" asked Jane, still thinking about the nanny. "The one who was wearing glasses and sniffed into a hanky?"

"Lugubrious," Tim said. "She sniffed all through the interview and wept at the end, when she told about her previous post."

"Whatever made her cry?" Jane asked.

"The child died of malnutrition," Tim explained. "She was describing its thinness and began to weep."

"Why didn't she feed it?"

"She forgot."

"How sad," Jane said.

"Father almost hired her. But then she told about the child's funeral. She spoke very reverently. Father is repulsed by reverence. Also, she dabbed her eyes. He dislikes dabbing."

"Look again if you would, Tim, and see if they've let this one in after that second ring," Barnaby A suggested.

Tim glanced down through the window. "Yes," he said. "She has entered. I'll go down into my spying place." He looked around the playroom. "Jane," he said, "you may continue your imaginative play with the doll."

Jane dutifully picked up her pencil and continued the note she was writing. I CANNOT CARE FOR MY POOR UGLY BABY, it said.

"A, read my book while I'm gone and be prepared to report on it to me. Chapter eleven," Tim said.

Barnaby A sighed. "But it's about thermodynamics," he said. "It's too hard."

Tim glared. "Is that a *whine?*" he asked. "Six-point deduction for whining." He turned to the other twin.

"You keep at those skyscraper windows, B," he said. "Ink them in. When you get to one hundred and twelve, we'll examine them carefully and determine whether the measurements are exact. If not, of course—"

Barnaby B nodded. "Yes, I know. We'll have to crumple." He glanced down at the nearby corner, where several previous skyscrapers—one had been very close to finished—lay crumpled.

"I'll report back shortly," Tim said, and left the playroom.

He returned five minutes later and the other Willoughby children all looked up in surprise. "You were very quick," Barnaby A commented, looking up from the book. "I have barely had time to learn anything about thermodynamics."

"And I was only up to the ninety-seventh window," Barnaby B said. "When you came back so suddenly, it startled me and I made a scribble."

"Crumple," ordered Tim, and Barnaby B crumpled his skyscraper sadly.

"He has hired her," Tim announced. "He did not conduct an interview. I think they were desperate. Father said, 'You're hired; there is your room,' and he pointed to the spare bedroom. She is already moving in. Her things will be sent by taxi."

"The spare bedroom is foul," Barnaby A pointed out.

"Yes, it has cockroaches," Barnaby B added.

"We don't care," Tim said. "*We* don't have to live in it."

"And Mother and Father?" asked Jane in a concerned tone. "When are they leaving?"

"They're gone. They had a cab waiting and they have left for the pier to board their ship."

"Without saying goodbye?" Jane asked, with a pitiful quaver in her voice.

"Jane," Tim told her, "I am taking *all* your points away. You have no points left because you had unrealistic expectations. Do you remember what happens to someone with no points?"

"Yes," Jane replied. "I have to stand in the corner with my hands neatly clasped." She went there and stood with her back to the room. The corner was a good place, actually, for thinking about how to become a more forceful and effective person.

"Now I will describe our new nanny," Tim said.

"May I listen?" asked the small voice from the corner.

"Yes, of course. In fact, you *must* listen. It's

required. There might be a quiz."

The two Barnabys sat side by side, listening attentively. Jane shifted from one foot to the other as she stood in the corner.

"I do not know her name," Tim began. "I expect she *has* a name, but I do not know it, and in any case we will never call her by it. Understand?"

His brothers and sister all nodded.

"She is heavyset," Tim said.

"Yes, I could see that from the window," Barnaby A murmured. Tim glared at him.

"She has now removed her hat. She has largeish ears. And gray hair badly arranged in a disorderly way."

"Oh dear," murmured Jane from the corner. Tim glared at her.

"She wears lace-up shoes and a man's watch that seems to be three minutes fast. Her legs are rather lumpy and I believe she has varicose veins. This is good. She will likely be unable to move fast."

"Weapons?" asked Barnaby A.

"None. Of course, we don't know what will be in her bags when they arrive. But there was nothing in her large purse but a folded apron. She has donned the apron."

"What's an apron?"

"It's a thing one wears to prevent stains on one's clothing. Owning an apron probably indicates that she is sloppy. And perhaps a poor cook."

"Mother was a vile cook," Barnaby B pointed out.

"True. So we won't worry about cooking quality. Anything will be better than Mother's."

"What *shall* we worry about, then?" Jane asked, turning slightly toward the room.

"I need to think about that," Tim said. "I'm sure there is something."

"She's not villainous?" asked Barnaby A.

"No."

"Or lugubrious?" asked Barnaby B.

"No."

"What, then?" asked Jane.

"Odious," Tim said. "She is an odious nanny."

# 6.
## NANNY PREPARES
## PORRIDGE

"Your room smells horrid," Jane said at breakfast, stirring her bowl of oatmeal as she looked at the nanny. "I could smell it when I came down the stairs."

"I could, too," said Barnaby A. "I had to use my asthma inhaler."

"It smells toxic," Tim pointed out. "And by the way, what is this hideous porridge you are serving us? Didn't our parents tell you that they only fed us eggs Benedict for breakfast? Or blueberry pancakes with whipped cream."

"They did *not*," Jane said, pleased at the forcefulness

in her own voice. "They always gave us hard-boiled eggs for breakfast. Sometimes the yellow part had turned green."

Tim glared at Jane and she resumed stirring.

The nanny turned and looked at them. Wearing her flowered apron, she was standing at the stove, stirring the oatmeal with a wooden spoon.

"I have fumigated my room with insecticide," she told them. "On the count of three, pinch your noses. Like this." She demonstrated, pinching her own nose with her left hand while she continued to stir with her right. "One. Two. Three."

The Willoughby children, startled by her command, all pinched their noses.

She looked at them. "Good," she said. "Now do that when you walk past my room. Otherwise you will breathe in phenolmethylcarbamate, and then you will die horribly. Writhing in pain.

"You may release your noses now," she added, noticing that they were still pinching. She spooned oatmeal into the boys' bowls and put them on the table.

"I have no wish to notify your parents of your deaths. Now eat your oatmeal. It has lots of soluble fiber."

"We disdain oatmeal," Tim told her.

"Starve, then," the nanny said.

"I like it if it has raisins," Jane said in a small voice, looking away from Tim's glare.

"I will add raisins tomorrow morning," the nanny said. "Thank you for mentioning that. I appreciate suggestions."

"Raisins are actually turds," Tim announced. Surprisingly, the other children paid no attention.

"Maybe a little sprinkling of brown sugar?" Barnaby A said to the nanny, after tasting his.

"Possibly. I'll give it some thought," she told him.

"Brown sugar is actually—" Tim began.

"Pipe down and eat," the nanny said.

"Oh my goodness, Nanny, you interrupted!" Jane said nervously. "Tim will take away some of your points."

"Points?" Nanny asked. "What are points?"

The children fell silent. They glanced apprehensively at Tim, who was sulkily moving his spoon around in his oatmeal.

"Well," Barnaby A began, "we each start out in the morning with fifty points. Then Tim takes points away if we interrupt—"

"Or whine," Jane added.

"Or argue, or obfuscate, or dawdle, or . . . I forget the rest," Barnaby B said.

"What happens at the end of the day, after the points are tallied?" Nanny asked with interest.

"Winner gets hot water in the bathtub," Jane said, "and losers have to use the leftover water. It's cold by then. And has soap scum." She gave a little shudder.

"Winner stays up as late as he wants," Barnaby A added. "Losers go to bed at seven."

"And can't read in bed," Barnaby B added sadly.

"Also," Jane began to say, "the winner—"

Nanny held up her hand in a STOP gesture. "I know all I need to know," she announced. "You each started out this morning with fifty points?"

The children nodded.

"Have you lost any yet?"

"Yes," Jane said. "I lost four points for yawning when I woke up. It was bad form."

"I lost nine for being a weakling and using my asthma inhaler," Barnaby A said.

"I broke my shoelace," his twin added. "That was five points off for clumsiness."

"Look at your bowls," Nanny commanded. They all did. Surprisingly, three of the bowls were empty.

"Three of you have eaten all of your oatmeal and

* * 38 * *

so I am giving you three each twenty extra points.

"*You*," she said, glaring at Tim, "are deducting twenty for not even tasting yours."

Hastily Tim took a bite of oatmeal.

She relented. "All right," she told him. "You may have five points back. And the rest if you finish it." Tim frowned and began to eat.

# 7.

## THE MELANCHOLY TYCOON

Let us turn our attention now to a mansion some distance away from the Willoughbys' tall, thin house. This is the Melanoff mansion, on the porch of which the Willoughby children had not long ago left a baby in a basket.

Mr. Melanoff—called Commander Melanoff for no particular reason except that he liked the sound of it—lived in squalor. Squalor is a situation in which there is moldy food in the refrigerator, mouse droppings are everywhere, the wastebaskets are over-flowing because they have not been emptied in weeks, and the washing machine stopped working months before—wet clothes within becoming moldy—but a repairman has never been summoned. There is a very bad smell to squalor.

Squalor has nothing to do with money. Squalor happens when people are sad. And Commander Melanoff was very sad.

He had made a vast fortune by manufacturing candy bars. His factory still existed, and the money kept coming in because people bought his hugely successful confections by the millions. But Commander Melanoff never went to his office anymore. He stayed in his squalorous mansion, where he moped and sulked.

He scowled as he ate his stale toast each morning, and he whimpered into his unheated canned soup at lunch. Each evening he dropped tears onto the pizza that was delivered to his porch by prearrangement, and each night he went to bed between his unwashed sheets and sobbed into his stained pillow. His mustache, once bristly and important-looking, was now dingy from grime and stiff from dried-up nose drippings.

He was sad because he had lost his wife. He had not actually been very fond of her. But it was sad, nonetheless, to be wifeless. She had been a dull but tidy and meticulous lady who had kept the house in perfect—almost *too* perfect—order. The commander's true, deep, unending sadness was because he had lost his only child, a small boy, while mother and son had been enjoying, without him, what had promised to be a lovely holiday. Their private railroad car had been buried by an avalanche near an Alpine village six years before, and crews of workers had been digging ever since through the towering piles of snow but had not yet uncovered the wreckage. For a long time Commander Melanoff had received a daily message about the progress of the search.

SEVEN INCHES TODAY BUT A BLIZZARD HAS HALTED OPERATIONS FOR THE TIME BEING, one message had reported.

ONLY TWO INCHES UNCOVERED TODAY DUE TO FOG AND SEVERAL UNFRIENDLY MOUNTAIN GOATS, said another.

The messages had come daily for a long time, then less frequently, but even now, after six years, were still slipped occasionally through the mail slot in his front door. He had stopped reading them years before. Each morning that a piece of mail with a Swiss postage stamp arrived, he whimpered, picked it up, and added it, unopened, to the stack in the corner that now reached an alarming height and had in places been shredded by mice making nests. Sometimes he looked mournfully at the stack and realized that his meticulous wife, had she not been lost in such a tragic way, would have sorted it, arranged it alphabetically, filed it by date and size and perhaps even by the color of the stamp. It made him nostalgic to think about how organized she—he found that he could not recall her name—had been.

But enough about sadness.

Something had happened. And now Commander Melanoff's life, surprisingly, was about to change.

One morning when he plodded into the hall to pick up the mail, he heard a sound from the porch. Of course there were often sounds from the world outside. But this was not the usual sound of squirrels gnawing on the wooden railings or pigeons strutting about on the rotting floorboards. He was familiar with those sounds and had ignored them for years.

This sound was different. It was a piteous wail. Commander Melanoff leaned over and poked open the mail slot with his index finger. He peered through and saw something amazing. He saw a stubbly-haired baby in a basket.

The baby, startled out of her pitiful wailing by the

sound of the brass flap to the mail slot opening, looked up and saw a thick, dirty mustache and above it a tear-filled eye gazing down at her in surprise.

She hiccupped and then smiled. Slowly the door opened.

# 8.
# A CRYPTIC COMMUNICATION

"Look at this," grumbled Tim. "They've survived so far." He was peering at the postcard that had arrived in the morning mail along with several bills and a poignant little note from a grandparent who was hoping to get a glimpse of the four children before they became adults.

He had thrown the rest of the mail away, but he had brought the postcard upstairs to the cobwebbed playroom. Now he was scowling at it.

"Thousands died in an earthquake but they only got bruised," he said with a groan. "We'll never be rid of them at this rate."

"May I see it?" asked Jane politely.

"No. It's too distressing for you."

"Could we?" the twins asked in unison. They cringed, knowing that points were deducted for speaking in unison, but Tim, distracted by the postcard, hadn't noticed.

"Have a quick look," Tim said, and held it toward them.

Barnaby A was an extremely fast reader. Although Tim whipped the postcard away from him quickly, he had been able to read it.

"I don't understand the part about the coal bin," he said.

"What about the coal bin?" Barnaby B asked. "I didn't read that far."

"Yes, what about the coal bin?" asked Jane. "I'm very scared of the coal bin."

Tim glared at her. "Five-point deduction for being a scaredy-cat," he announced. "I'll read the stupid postcard aloud."

"'Dear ones,'" Tim read. "'Though slightly bruised, we have survived quite a lovely earthquake (you may have read the headlines: THOUSANDS KILLED) . . .'"

"Oh my," Jane said sadly. "I suppose kittens were killed, too. How sad."

"Shhh," Tim told her, and he continued. "'. . . and

next we are off to kayak a crocodile-infested river. Such FUN!'"

"They don't know how to kayak!" Barnaby A exclaimed.

"They never once have kayaked!" his twin added.

"Precisely," Tim said.

"May I ask a question?" Jane asked timidly. Tim, still holding the postcard, nodded.

"I'm wondering," Jane said, "would a crocodile eat a person in one gulp? Or in chunks?"

Her three brothers all thought for a minute.

"Chunks," said Barnaby A.

"Chunks," said Barnaby B.

"Yes, large chunks," Tim said decisively. "Gulping down chunks for the nourishment, but quickly, to avoid the taste. The same way we eat Mother's meat loaf."

*"Ate,"* Jane pointed out. "Nanny's meat loaf is quite good."

Tim glared at her briefly. "Continuing," he announced, and held up the card. "'We hope the nanny is earning her salary,'" he read aloud. "Now this next part," he said, "I don't understand. 'Please hide in the coal bin if prospective buyers come to look at the house.'"

"What are prospective buyers? I'm scared of the

coal bin," Jane said again. "Remember when you made me stay down there because I whined, and there were *rats?*"

"I know! I know what it means!" Barnaby A said eagerly, raising his hand so that he would be allowed to speak.

"Yes, we both know!" his twin said. "We just saw the sign!"

"What sign?" asked Tim.

"Look outside! It's on a window box!"

Tim went to the playroom window and looked down at the two boxes filled with begonias that were attached to the first-floor windows. "I can see there is some sort of sign," he acknowledged. "What does it say?"

"FOR SALE!" the twins announced.

"We're for sale?" Jane asked in surprise.

"No, dodo," Tim said. "Apparently our *house* is."

"And it says CHEAP!" Barnaby B added.

"So," Tim mused, "while we're getting rid of *them*, they're getting rid of *us*."

"Complicated," said Barnaby A.

"Diabolical," said Barnaby B.

"Scary," said Jane.

"Despicable," said Tim. "Absolutely despicable."

# 9.
## CLEVER CAMOUFLAGE

The woman at the door handed Tim a card that said her name and explained that she was a real estate agent. "I'll be by in an hour with a prospective buyer," she told him, "and I know your parents have explained that you children must remain out of sight while I show the house.

"Remember that," she said sternly, shaking her finger. "One hour from now. Out of sight."

"Oh dear," wailed Jane when he told them, "does that mean the coal bin? I just can't bear the coal bin!"

Tim thought it over. "She only said 'out of sight.' She didn't say 'coal bin' specifically."

"If only we could make ourselves invisible," Barnaby A remarked.

"Yes, we have a comic called *Invisible Man!*" his twin reminded him. "If we could just do that!"

"I have a better idea, actually," Tim announced. "We will camouflage ourselves."

"What's that?" asked Jane. "Does it hurt?"

"No, dodo. It means we make ourselves blend in so that no one will notice us."

"We have toy soldiers in camouflage outfits!" Barnaby A remembered. "The cat chewed them, so they're ruined now," he added sadly.

"Quiet. We don't have much time. Five minutes have already passed." Tim looked at the other children carefully. "A?" he said. "You're easy because you're wearing the sweater today."

"Yes, it's Wednesday. I always wear the sweater on Wednesdays."

"Hold up your arms," Tim instructed him. "Like this."

Tim demonstrated, holding each arm out and bent, as if someone were aiming a gun at him. Barnaby A imitated him. The overly long sweater sleeves flopped over his hands.

"Good," said Tim, examining his pose. "Now pull the neck of the sweater up over your head,"

Tim said, and Barnaby A did so.

"Excellent. Relax for a minute now. Then get that largish wastebasket from Father's study and stand in it, in your pose."

Barnaby A did so. They all looked at him, and Tim said, "Perfect. You are camouflaged as a cactus. Place yourself in a corner of the dining room, and when the doorbell rings, announcing the prospective buyer, assume your pose. Choose a place by a sunny window. Cacti prefer sun."

"What if someone tries to water me or test my prickers?" Barnaby A asked in a muffled voice.

"They won't," replied Tim. "I am setting up a notice that says: STAY AWAY. THIS HIGHLY POISONOUS CACTUS EMITS TOXIC FUMES."

"Might I be a cactus, too?" Jane asked, watching as Barnaby A, sweater sleeves dangling, went off to the dining room with his wastebasket.

"No, dodo. You will be a lamp. Here. Let me just look in this closet . . ." Tim went to the hall closet and stood on tiptoe to find something on a high shelf. "Good. She left it behind. Here you are, Jane." He opened a large hatbox and handed Jane their mother's going-to-church hat, which was dark brown straw in the shape of a bowl.

"Kneel on that table there, beside the sofa," Tim directed his sister. She climbed up and knelt on the table.

"It hurts my knees," Jane whimpered.

Tim thought it over. "All right," he said. "Squat. And hunch."

Jane squatted and hunched.

"Good. Here's your lampshade," Tim said. He lowered the large hat onto her head. It covered her face.

"I can't see!" Jane said in a worried voice.

"Lamps don't need to see," Tim replied. "When the doorbell rings, assume that pose and hold very still while the prospective buyer comes through."

Jane lifted her shade slightly and peered out. "What if someone tries to turn me on?" she asked nervously.

"Good thought, Jane!" Tim said. "I'm going to give you ten points today, for thinking of that possibility!

"And I give myself twenty points," he added, "for finding the solution." He went to his father's desk, used a pen and paper, and returned to the table where Jane was still kneeling, with a note in his hand.

THE ELECTRICITY IN THIS HOUSE IS DEFECTIVE AND MAY ELECTROCUTE YOU IF YOU TURN ON A LAMP, said the note that Tim had printed. He placed it by Jane's feet. "When they come through," he told her, "hold very still. Don't let that shade wobble. And make yourself as thin as possible."

"How much time do we have?" Barnaby B asked uneasily. "I don't have a camouflage yet. I wish it had been my day for the sweater."

"Don't be a worrywart, B," Tim said. "Come out here to the hall. Stand there by the door and hold your arms up."

Barnaby B did so, and Tim hung overcoats, taken from the hall closet, over his arms. "There," he said. "You are a coat tree."

"Will people fling coats over me? I might sneeze — or suffocate," Barnaby B said.

"No one will. I will prepare a notice that says: THE FURNACE IN THIS HOUSE IS DEFECTIVE. WEAR YOUR COAT. DO NOT HANG UP YOUR COAT OR YOU WILL FREEZE."

"But my face shows," Barnaby B complained.

Tim took his father's felt hat, the one he wore to the bank each day, and hung it over Barnaby B's face. "There," he said.

"It doesn't smell nice," Barnaby B said in a muffled voice.

"That's because of the sweatband," Tim explained.

"All men's hats have sweatbands inside. They smell nasty. Just hold your breath and you won't notice. Now: practice being motionless, all of you," he called, so that they could hear him in the other rooms.

It was silent as the children remained motionless in their poses. Tim went to the closet again.

"Tim?" called a voice from the dining room. It was the cactus.

"Tim?" called the coat tree from the hall.

"Tim?" the lamp called from its table.

"What?" Tim's voice was muffled.

"What are you going to be?" asked the cactus.

"Where will you be, Tim?" asked the lamp.

"What is your camouflage, Tim?" asked the coat tree.

From the floor in front of the living room fireplace, Tim replied. "I am wrapped in Mother's mink coat!" he called, his voice still muffled by the fur. "I am camouflaged as a fur rug!"

"What if someone steps on you, Tim?" the lamp asked in a worried voice.

"I would be very brave and very silent and completely immobile no matter how bad the pain," he replied. "However, it is unlikely. I have set up a notice that says: THE FLOOR UNDER THIS RUG IS ROTTEN. IF YOU STEP ON THIS RUG YOU WILL FALL INTO THE BASEMENT AND BE DESPERATELY INJURED. Now hush. I hear someone on the front steps."

The camouflaged Willoughbys all fell silent. They heard the front door open and the voice of the woman Tim had met an hour before. She was speaking now to the prospective buyer.

"This is a beautifully decorated home," she said. "Such good taste. Please come in and hang up your coat. I'll show you around."

# 10.
## An Alabaster Aphrodite

"I'm amazed that you children don't emerge dirtier from the coal bin," Nanny said. "I expected I'd have to bathe you all and launder your clothes after prospective buyers were here. But each time you reappear quite clean."

They were seated at the supper table, eating succulent pot roast; nearby, on the counter, was the still warm pie they would have for dessert. Nanny, it had turned out, was an outstanding cook. Even her morning oatmeal, now that she added raisins and brown sugar, was delicious.

Four prospective buyers had been through the house by now, but no one had shown an interest in buying it. Each one left looking puzzled, murmuring comments about the odd plants and rugs and lamps and furniture and expressing concern over toxic air, bad wiring, a broken furnace, and rotten floorboards.

"We're very careful," Tim explained. "We have found ways to stay out of sight and remain clean."

"I'm a lamp," Jane said.

"You are indeed, dear," said Nanny, leaning over to wipe a bit of gravy from Jane's chin. "A real little lamb."

"I'm a cactus," Barnaby A said.

Nanny had gone to the counter to get the pie. She turned and said fondly, "Practice? I didn't know you played an instrument, dear. Where do you practice? You're very quiet."

"I'm a coat tree," Barnaby B said with a frown.

Nanny sliced the pie neatly into triangular-shaped pieces. She slid each one onto a small plate. "Poetry?" she said with a smile. "You are poetry? Well, I wouldn't say that, exactly, but it's a lovely thought, isn't it?" She took the children's empty dinner plates away and began to pass the pie around.

"Where do *you* go, Nanny, when prospective

buyers come?" asked Barnaby A. "You reappear quite clean as well."

Nanny blushed. "Oh, I don't want to say, really."

"Tell," Tim commanded, "or we won't eat your pie. Do you camouflage yourself?"

"I guess you could say that," Nanny replied. "The pie is raspberry, by the way."

"Are you a rug? Or a coat tree?" asked Barnaby B. "A lamp? Or maybe a cactus?"

Nanny took a bite of raspberry pie and chewed, with a satisfied look. Then she announced in a prim, educational voice, "I'm a statue. I do this." After setting her fork down on the plate, she got up from her chair and stood beside the stove, where she created a pose with both arms behind her head and one hip jutting forward. "I stand in the upstairs hall, next to the linen closet."

"But you don't look one bit like a statue, Nanny!" Tim pointed out. "You're wearing a flowered apron, elastic stockings, and lace-up shoes."

"*Now* who's being a dodo!" Nanny told Tim. "Of course I don't wear these things. We have plenty of warning before prospective buyers come. As soon as we are notified, I rush to my room and remove my shoes, stockings, apron, and all the rest. I powder myself with talc to look like alabaster."

"What's alabaster?" asked Jane.

"White," Tim told her. "Like marble."

"When I'm posing," Nanny went on, "I believe I look very much like Aphrodite."

"Who's Aphrodite?" asked Jane.

"Daughter of Zeus. Also known as Venus. But the most famous statue of Venus has no arms. I have arms." She held them up. "So I think of myself as Aphrodite when I am posing as a statue."

"You mean you're *naked,* Nanny?" Barnaby A asked in amazement.

"Statues are never naked," Nanny said in a somewhat shocked voice. "They are *nude.* Anyway, I drape myself. I use a sheet."

"So," Barnaby B said, poking his fork into a piece of raspberry pie, "you stand there nude, except for the sheet, and all powdered, and in a pose, and perfectly still?"

"Well," Nanny admitted, "sometimes I wink."

"The other day, that prospective buyer who ran downstairs screaming?" Tim asked. "Was that because you winked?"

"Possibly," Nanny replied very primly.

They were all silent for a moment, picturing the

scene. The prospective buyer had looked truly horrified and had run shrieking through the front door and not been seen since.

"What's that noise?" Barnaby B said suddenly. "I hear something banging!"

"It's at the front of the house," Jane said, listening. "Someone is hammering."

After a moment the noise ceased. They all went to look. More words had been added to the sign that was tacked to the window box.

"*Reduced? Cheaper?* This house is never going to be sold," Tim murmured.

"I can't imagine why not," said Nanny, smiling in an Aphrodite-like way.

# 11.
## An Astonishing acquisition

Commander Melanoff opened the door and peered into the basket in astonishment. He looked up and down the street to see if a delivery man had left this ... this ... this *thing* on his doorstep by mistake.

But no. The street was quite empty. Finally, in confusion because it kept *smiling* at him and no one had smiled at him in a very long time, he leaned down and lifted it out of its basket. Holding it at arm's length because its lower half was damp, Commander Melanoff carried the stubbly-haired baby into his mansion.

He looked around for a suitable place to set it down. The velvet couch in the drawing room had holes in it that mice had made, and gray wads of stuffing were protruding from the holes. There was a table nearby, but an old, opened pizza box with some greenish pizza crusts inside had been on the table for weeks. Ants were crawling on it.

Finally he carried the creature into the kitchen and laid it carefully on the drain board beside the sink. From his half-forgotten past, thinking back sadly to his own lost child, he vaguely remembered the procedure about diapers. In a nearby drawer, reaching with one arm while he kept the other firmly upon the wriggling infant, he located a folded dishtowel. He had not washed dishes in several years. He had thrown some away after they had been used, and others he had reused, simply heaping his takeout Chinese food or pizza slices onto the remains of the last meal. So there was still a drawer filled with laundered dishtowels, left over from the days when there had been cooks and servants in the large kitchen, the days when his wife had organized things like dishtowels by color and size and date of purchase. He fashioned one into a sort of diaper and tied it awkwardly around the bottom half of the baby. Then, holding the baby in one arm, he opened the large refrigerator and peered inside.

Once, long ago, this refrigerator had been filled with juices and jams, casseroles and chickens, cheeses and pastries, salad greens and truffles and endives and olives. It had always been a little distressing to him that his meticulous wife had insisted on alphabetical arrangements. It meant that ascots were next to argyle socks in his dresser, and his underwear was tucked away with the umbrellas. Even here, in the kitchen, one had had to locate the anchovies in order to find the apricots. Still, he thought wistfully, it had been pleasing to have the refrigerator filled with food.

Now it was completely empty except for a small bowl with something green and furry on the bottom and a stack of test candy bars for his factory. He had been, before his tragedy, working on a new bar filled with caramel and nuts in various combinations and coated with rich chocolate. He had thought, then, that it would be his masterpiece. Now the test bars, turning gray with age, lay in uneven stacks on a refrigerator shelf. He groaned slightly when he saw them and closed the heavy door.

He reached for the telephone, balanced it on his

shoulder, and dialed the number of the local grocery store and pizza parlor.

"This is Commander Melanoff," he said when the grocer answered. "Deliver milk immediately, and, ah . . ." —he glanced at the baby,— "oatmeal, I think. Yes, oatmeal. Maybe applesauce.

"And things to wrap around the bottom of an infant. Not dishtowels."

"Pampers?" asked the grocer.

"I am an old-fashioned gentleman."

"Diapers, then?" suggested the grocer. "Or, if you are truly old-fashioned, they would be called nappies."

"Yes, those."

"Anything else, sir?"

"Oh, dear." Commander Melanoff whimpered a bit. "I don't know."

"Have you acquired an infant, sir?"

The commander sighed. "Yes," he acknowledged.

"What size, sir?"

The melancholy tycoon looked down at it. He remembered holiday celebrations of the past. "The size of a small turkey," he said.

"That would be about fourteen to sixteen pounds, I'd say. Does it have teeth, sir?"

Cradling the telephone again on his shoulder, Commander Melanoff gingerly used his free hand to pry open the small mouth so that he could look inside. "A few," he said. "Three, I think. And very stubbly hair."

"Does it appear capable of chewing, sir?"

At that moment the baby bit down on Commander Melanoff's finger.

"Ouch! Yes, it does," he said into the telephone.

"Very good, sir. Our delivery boy will be there shortly with everything you need. And shall we send tonight's pizza at the same time?"

Gloomily Commander Melanoff looked around the kitchen. The remains of at least twenty-three pizzas—old crusts dotted with decaying pepperoni slices—and their torn-open, stained boxes were stacked on countertops and tables everywhere. Then he looked at the infant still in his arms. She smiled up at him.

"No," he told the grocer with a sigh. "Send a salad and some vitamins. I think I'm going to have to reinvigorate myself.

"Send soap as well," he added reluctantly, before he hung up. "I am going to need soap." Then he replaced the telephone receiver. He stared down again at the thing in his arms. The placid baby stared back, then reached up and tugged gently at his mustache.

* * *

And so life began anew for the melancholy tycoon and the affable infant. He called her Ruth, since he had eventually unfolded and read the note that had been pinned to her clothing. "Her name is Ruth," the note had said. He ordered clothes for her, since it would have made him too sad to go to the attic and open the trunks and boxes that contained small clothing that had been his own child's.

And, too, his own lost child had been a son. This one was a girl. So he bought small, elegant velvet dresses and pinafores with lace. He bought hair ribbons, though the baby's hair was oddly stubbly and short and there was nothing to tie a ribbon to; he hoped it would grow.

On the advice of an elderly saleslady at the expensive store at which he had placed his order, he also bought more serviceable clothing: overalls and jump suits with small pockets and appliquéd giraffes. "A baby needs to play," the woman had told him. "The little dresses are fine for birthday parties and Christmas photographs. But she will need to crawl on the floor and explore. Let me recommend these very fine play clothes. Shall I add them to your bill?" And he had said yes.

"We could monogram everything," she added. "A monogram is a very fine thing."

Commander Melanoff knew what a monogram was. In the days when he had gone each morning to his factory, he had worn shirts with his initials hand-embroidered on the pocket.

"I don't know her initials," he explained sadly to the saleslady.

"Oh, dear. Do you know her name?"

"Ruth."

"Lovely. Why don't we embroider 'Ruth' on all her clothes, then? A short name suits that purpose so well. If her name were, say, Clementina, then we would have to rethink, wouldn't we? Monograms are charged by the letter. Clementina would be very costly."

"Money is of no importance. I want the best," he replied.

And so all of her clothing was adorned with her name.

He cleaned the house on behalf of Ruth's well-being. He carried all the pizza boxes to the trash and washed the mouse droppings from the countertops and the floors. But when she crawled across the newly cleaned living room floor and grabbed the edge of the elegant draperies, swirls of dust arose and moths that had been living in the deep folds of fabric were dislodged and flew in confusion around the room. Ruth laughed at the sight of the fluttering insects, but Commander Melanoff took down the heavy draperies and added them to the pile of trash, on top of the pizza boxes. He called in fumigators to rid the house of moths; then he washed the windows, which had become so caked with grime that the neighborhood was blurred.

The only thing he did not clean or dislodge as he went about his work with brooms and sweepers and buckets and brushes was the towering stack of unopened mail from Switzerland, the six years of messages and telegrams and letters that were still piled against the wall of the front hall.

Ruth, who was still acquiring teeth, occasionally pulled a bit of paper from the lower portion of the stack and chewed on it. One morning Commander Melanoff, who had prepared the baby's morning oatmeal in the kitchen, picked her up from where she was happily crawling on the hall floor. She spat a scrap of yellowing paper into his hand.

He looked at the torn words and phrases and groaned, remembering those early days when he had still had hope.

Carefully he tied a bib around her neck to protect her pink hand-smocked monogrammed jump suit. "There you are, Baby Ruth," he said, and sat her in the highchair he had ordered from a costly catalog. Spooning the oatmeal into her mouth, he thought about the stack of mail. He decided that he must throw it all away. But time passed, and he could not bring himself to do it.

Often the baby played in the hall, and sometimes she grabbed at the letters. In her first weeks with Commander Melanoff, she could reach only the earliest mail. But when she began to pull herself up and stand on wobbly legs, she reached higher. Once she withdrew a sealed envelope with a Swiss stamp from the middle of the stack. She tore the envelope open, removed a folded letter, and chewed on it briefly.

Then she crumpled the damp paper into a ball and rolled it across the floor for the cat to chase.

The cat could not read, for it was a cat. Ruth could not read, for she was a baby. Commander Melanoff, who was a grown man with several college degrees, could read extremely well but never noticed the wad of paper that eventually wedged itself under a radiator. So no one knew that a letter mailed four years earlier had announced, "THEY ARE FOUND ALIVE!"

# 12.
## ANOTHER CRYPTIC
## COMMUNICATION

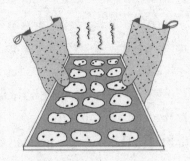

"They survived the crocodiles," Tim announced glumly, entering the kitchen and holding up another postcard.

"Let's see! What does it say?" Jane and the twins wiped their hands quickly and rushed over to see. They had all been helping Nanny bake some cookies, a very old-fashioned thing to do.

Tim held it out and began to read it aloud.

"'Dear ones,'" he read.

"I wonder why they call us dear ones when they're trying to sell us," Barnaby A said, looking puzzled.

Nanny added raisins to the bowl of dough. "It's a nicety," she explained, stirring.

"They're just pretending, aren't they, Nanny?" asked Jane.

"Yes, dear. Hand me those chopped nuts, please."

Jane passed the measuring cup filled with chopped pecans to Nanny. "They don't really like us, do they, Nanny?" she asked.

"No, dear. They told me that when they hired me."

"What did they say? Did they call us terrible names?" Barnaby B asked with interest.

Nanny paused in her stirring. "Let me think. It seems so long ago, I've almost forgotten. They called you—oh, what was it?"

"Odious?" asked Tim. "That's what I called *you*, Nanny."

"No, not odious. They called you insufferable, Tim. 'The eldest is insufferable,' they said. They couldn't remember your name."

"And us? What did they call us?" the twins asked together.

"Repetitious," Nanny told them. "They said you were repetitious and tedious because they couldn't tell you apart. And your mother said you were greedy because you wanted two sweaters.

"I'm sorry I don't know how to knit, boys," Nanny added apologetically, "or I'd make you another sweater. I do think it would be nice if you each had one."

"Me?" asked Jane in a small voice. "What did they say about me?"

"They forgot you, dear. I was actually quite surprised after they left and I settled in and found four children. They had told me they had three."

"Were you glad?" Jane asked, a little nervously.

Nanny wrinkled her nose. "Well, I was sorry I hadn't asked for a higher salary. I usually charge more for four children.

"But it was lovely to find a little girl," she added. "I do like little girls."

She began to form the cookie dough into balls and dropped them one by one onto a baking sheet. "Would you go on, please, Tim? About the crocodiles?"

Tim turned back to the postcard. But before he began reading again he looked up and said, "That's heinous, Nanny, that they didn't tell you about Jane. They cheated you out of some of your salary. I always knew they were cheaters. Father always tried to shortchange me on my allowance. I had to count carefully every week."

"You got an *allowance?*" asked Barnaby A with a surprised look. "We never got an allowance!"

"Never!" added Barnaby B.

"What's an allowance?" asked Jane piteously.

"Never mind," Nanny soothed. "That time is past. I believe that we would all benefit, actually, if they were to be eaten by crocodiles. There is a provision in their will that I am to continue taking care of you if tragedy befalls them. And you, of course, would all be rich.

"Homeless, though," she added, "if a buyer comes along and wants the house."

"No one will," Tim said confidently. "Here. I'll read this now.

"'The crocodile river was such fun. Two tourists were eaten in huge gulps but it was not sad at all because they were French. Father and I fought the creatures off with our kayak paddles and triumphed. Tomorrow we are taking a helicopter trip over an erupting volcano. We got quite a bargain because the pilot has not completed his training. MUCH more expensive to have an experienced pilot! By the way, when the house is sold and you move elsewhere, would you leave your clothes behind? We will take them to the secondhand shop and get a commission.'"

The four children and Nanny were all silent for a moment. Then Nanny tilted the bowl toward the children.

"Here. Lick."

One by one they scraped the raw dough from the bowl with their fingers and then licked. Nanny herself licked the wooden spoon with which she had stirred. The smell of the baking cookies began to emanate from the oven, fragrant and warm.

"Tim?" said Nanny.

"What?"

"Will you give me some extra points if I have a very fine suggestion?"

"Well," Tim replied, "I've kind of stopped my point system. I would have given you a whole lot of points for the bowl licking, but I'd forgotten all about the system.

"What's your suggestion, though?" he asked.

"It's somewhat diabolical," Nanny said, guiltily.

"Tell," said all the children together.

"We could find that secondhand shop and sell *their* clothes," Nanny said.

"We could," agreed Tim, "but not *all* their clothes. I still need Mother's mink coat, even though it's hot and weighs a ton."

"And I still need Mother's large hat, even though I can't see when it's on my head," said Jane.

"And I still need Father's hat with the sweatband," Barnaby B added, "even though it smells nasty."

"Eventually, when we are quite sure they're gone, we can sell all their clothes," Tim decided.

"Oh," said Jane in an imploring voice, "*do* let's wish for a helicopter-and-volcano disaster!"

They all took a deep breath, closed their eyes, and wished fervently. Then Nanny took the freshly baked cookies from the oven, poured five glasses of milk, and sat down with the children at the table.

# 13.
## THE OBSEQUIOUS POSTMASTER

Far away, in a small village in northwest Switzerland, the postmaster was diligently sorting the incoming mail, as he did every morning. He was a tall, thin man with a jutting chin and large, clumsy hands. His name was Hans-Peter von Schlusseldorf. He lived alone in the village with his dog, Horst, who came with him each morning to work and who now lay snoring on the floor of the tiny post office.

*"Ach!"* exclaimed the postmaster in frustration as once again he dropped several letters onto the wooden floor. Horst opened one eye, yawned, then rose to his large feet, ambled over, picked up the

dropped letters with his mouth, and gave them back to the postmaster.

*"Danke,"* the postmaster said to the dog. He was grateful for the help because it was difficult for him to bend. He had been frozen solid once, years before, while climbing a nearby mountain, and though he had been successfully thawed after his rescue, his joints remained stiff. With the retrieved mail back in his hand, he continued his sorting. The wall behind him was lined with postal boxes—it was where the village inhabitants collected their mail. One by one he added letters to the small boxes.

The tiny bell at the top of the door rang as a woman entered with her little boy. He recognized her because she came each day for her mail, though she rarely received anything except her utility bills and an occasional advertising brochure.

*"Guten Tag, Frau—"* He began to greet her in his usual friendly fashion, then remembered the language situation. This woman spoke only English. He corrected himself. "I mean, good morning." He glanced toward the box in the "M" section, remembering her initial. But "M" was empty. "No mail for you, I'm afraid, but I have not finished my sorting yet, so perhaps you will wait?"

He hoped she would. He was a bachelor, after all, and this was a lone woman, not unattractive. Tall and thin, like himself. And a little mysterious. Hans-Peter liked mysteries. All he knew about this woman was that she had been buried within a luxurious railroad car for years by an avalanche, with her child, but had survived. He had heard that when the rescuers finally reached her, she was wearing a silk dress, had her hair curled and combed, and was sipping tea while she read a book about whales. Her first words upon the rescue, he had heard, were, "Thank goodness. I have read this book forty-two times and every other one even more often than that."

Feeling that it would be rude not to include her child in his greeting (though in truth he did not much like children), the postmaster turned to the boy and repeated his "good morning."

"He speaks German," the woman said.

The postmaster smiled painfully and said, *"Guten Tag,"* to the boy. His smile was pained because he had heard the boy try to speak what he thought was German. He simply used English words and added extra syllables with a vaguely Germanic sound.

"Helloschlimhofen," the boy said cheerfully. "Neisch day, isn't itzenschlitz?"

Everyone in the village thought it would be rude to point out the flawed German and help the child to learn the language correctly. The Swiss are scrupulously polite. Even the schoolmaster, who taught all the village children, including this strange little boy who had spent his formative years in a buried train car, simply ignored the odd attempt at language. At least the child was good at math.

The woman was looking at the postal boxes somewhat critically. "Your filing system leaves much to be desired. You put an 'S' into the 'C' box—I expect it was a clumsy error. In addition, the envelopes are not aligned well. They should be straightened thusly." She walked briskly behind the counter, removed several letters, lined them up by the corners, tapped them on the countertop to perfect the alignment, and then replaced them in the box.

"I can certainly see the difference, madam," the postmaster said. "Thank you." He did admire the woman's skill with her hands and the quickness with which she was now organizing the boxes. He found himself thinking that he liked her hair as well, the way it fell around her shoulders in soft, luxuriant waves. And her lips! The redness, the moistness, of them!

He turned away, embarrassed at his own thoughts. "Do you need any stamps today, *Frau*?" he asked. "Or should I call you Mrs.?"

"It's Ms.," she replied. "Or in your language I expect it is, what? *Fräulein*?" She chuckled slightly and straightened the fingers of her gloves carefully because there was a small wrinkle at one knuckle and wrinkles made her very nervous and fretful.

"It would be *Frau*," he said politely, almost bowing, "because you are a married woman." His heart almost broke as he said those words. If only—!

"No, Postmaster von Schlusseldorf, I am not," she said.

"I beg your pardon, madam, but for many years I have been mailing off letters, some marked urgent, to Herr Melanoff. Before you were found, I sent the letters from the rescue workers. Some were so sad. I remember a day when they thought they had located you but it proved to be only the rusted remains of a snowplow that was buried back in 1949. Such hopes dashed! 'Disappointing news for her husband,' they told me that day, I remember. I believe it was four years ago."

"Ex-husband," the woman announced in a clipped voice.

Could it be? Dare he hope? The postmaster placed his hand over his heart, which beat nervously under his blue uniform. "I see. Perhaps I misunderstood, madam."

"Darling," she said (and the postmaster's heart leaped, but then he realized it was her son to whom she spoke), "stand up straight so that your trouser lengths are not mismatched. It makes me very nervous when things are not in order."

The boy, who had been sprawled on the floor patting the dog, stood up straight at his mother's command. He was not wearing trousers, exactly, but the postmaster did not want to correct her. The boy was wearing lederhosen, short leather pants that were common among the folk villages of Switzerland. Below the lederhosen, his knees were thin and knobby. High woolen socks encased his lower legs.

"Itz that better, Mutti? Neitz und schtraight?"

"You know I don't speak German, dear," she replied.

"Ach. I forgotzenplunkt. Sorrybrauten," the boy said. "Are my pant legs nice and straight now?"

She examined him and nodded. "Yes. Try to stand with your weight evenly distributed, won't you, dear? And adjust your shirt collar." She then told her son,

"I was just explaining to the postmaster that I am no longer married." She glanced toward the counter where Hans-Peter stood.

"After all these years of no reply from my boy's father, dear Herr von Schlusseldorf—and who knows that better than you? such a long-lasting silence from Commander Melanoff!—your kindly Swiss laws have allowed me to resume my single status."

"And so—" the postmaster stammered.

"Yes. I am available," she said to him. "Please smoothe your lapel; it's a little mussed. And see if perhaps tomorrow morning, when you shave, you could even those sideburns? I believe the right one is a fraction shorter than the left."

"Yes, of course! Thank you for bringing it to my attention!"

"Come along now, son." She turned to the boy. "I want to be at the market at precisely five minutes past ten. We're already twenty seconds behind."

How he loved a woman who was so precise, just like a Swiss train coming into a station! Hans-Peter allowed himself to hope, for the first time in his life, for a future that might perhaps include a postmistress! He bowed to her, clicking his heels slightly, and she nodded a polite goodbye.

"Schlee you later, alligatorplatz!" the boy said. "Bye-bye, Horstwurst!" he added, speaking to the dog. Then he followed his mother out of the post office and into the village's main street.

Watching the woman's tall, straight back as she walked toward the market, the postmaster fingered his sideburns and planned his next morning's meticulous shave with a shiver of excitement.

# 14.
## REENCOUNTERING
## AN INFANT

Nanny and the Willoughbys were out for a walk. This was something that old-fashioned families did from time to time, to expose themselves to invigorating fresh air. Nanny had donned her blue cape, which was the official uniform for nannies.

"Walk briskly, children," said Nanny, "and swing your arms."

They did so.

"Skip, if you like," Nanny said. "Skipping is very healthful."

"What is skipping?" Jane asked.

"Yes, what is skipping?" asked the twins.

"It's like this, dolts," Tim told them, and he skipped ahead of them to demonstrate.

"No more saying of the word *dolt*," Nanny announced. "I dislike it."

"What about *dodo*?" Jane asked.

"Well, let's allow *dodo* for now," Nanny said after thinking it over. "If someone does something *really* stupid, it is permissible to call that person a dodo.

"And," she added, looking at Tim, who had returned, "if you think that was skipping, you are a dodo. *This* is skipping."

She demonstrated, skipping to the corner of the block with her cape flying behind her. She turned and beckoned to the children, and they skipped toward her one by one. Nanny gave some further instructions— *a little more left foot, Tim; no timidity, go flat out, A; good job, much better than before, B*—and a pat on the back for Jane, who stumbled and skinned her knee but was heroically not crying.

Now, having walked for several blocks and skipped for the last one, the children found that they were on a familiar street. They had not been back to this street since the day they had trudged here hauling a wagon containing a basket with a baby in it. Tim nudged Barnaby A and nodded meaningfully toward the mansion that loomed ahead. Both of the twins gave nervous glances but then looked away and concentrated on remarks about the quality of the asphalt in the street and a particularly odd-shaped cloud in the sky. Jane fell silent and had a sad look. She had *liked* the baby, actually, though when its hair was cropped she had found it homely. From time to time she had missed it and wondered about it.

Nanny skipped ahead, not noticing that a hush had fallen upon the children.

"The windows are repaired," Barnaby B pointed out in a whisper.

"And the cat has been fed," his twin noticed. "It was thin before, but now it's pudgy."

"Someone has mowed the lawn," Tim observed.

"Shhhh," said Jane suddenly. "I hear a giggle."

They stood still, the four of them, and after a moment Nanny returned. She had skipped the entire length of the block, assuming the children were behind her. Now she came back to see why they had stopped. "The important thing in terms of fresh-air intake," Nanny said to them, "is continuity! If you stop, you lose your continuity. Why ever are you standing about like dodos? You are breathing stagnant air."

The children shifted their feet and didn't reply. Tim began to hum a bit. The twins stared at the pavement.

"What's that sound?" Nanny asked suddenly.

"I'm just humming 'The Battle Hymn of the Republic,'" Tim explained. "I try to do it in its entirety twice a day. Usually no one hears me. Sometimes I do it in the bathroom. It is possible to hum while brushing one's teeth."

"No, no. I meant *that* sound." Nanny held up one finger to silence them, and now they could all hear the delicious giggle from the porch of the mansion.

"I think we should go home," Barnaby A said nervously.

"Yes, isn't it lunchtime? Weren't you planning vichyssoise for lunch, Nanny?" asked Barnaby B.

"Let's skip home!" suggested Tim. He did a few tentative moves of his feet and arms.

"It's a very sweet sound," Jane said, glancing at Nanny.

"It's a baby!" Nanny announced. "On the porch of that mansion! Let's go look!"

"I believe," Tim said, "that it is quite against the law to enter a private gate and cross a private walk and ascend the steps of a private porch. I think we might very well be arrested, Nanny, if we investigate this any further. Let's leave at once. Fifty points off anyone who does not leave immediately."

"Nonsense," said Nanny. "You stopped that silly point thing weeks ago. Come. Close the gate behind you in case there is a dog confined in the yard. I once knew someone whose spaniel fled when a gate was left open and it was never seen again and three members of the family died of grief."

Jane took Nanny's hand and followed her through the gate. "I do love babies," Jane confided. "I've always wanted one. I remember when we found—"

Tim interrupted her. "I don't believe people die of grief," he muttered. He came through the gate as well and latched it behind him. Only the twins remained on the sidewalk, looking nervous.

"Yes, they do," Nanny told him. "They waste away. I have known at least twelve people who have died of grief. It's a terrible way to go."

"It is indeed!" a loud voice suddenly said. All of them, even Nanny, jumped.

A large man with a thick mustache had appeared suddenly through a door that opened onto the porch. He was wearing a tweed jacket and a polka-dot bow tie, and he was carrying a box of cookies.

"I myself came very close to dying of grief not

long ago," he announced. "How do you do—I am Commander Melanoff. What are you doing on my porch? Have a ginger cookie?"

Nanny took one. "We heard a lovely giggle from your porch and came to investigate. I have learned over the course of my many years that it is a bad idea, usually, to investigate piteous weeping but always a fine thing to look into a giggle." She bit into the cookie. "Delicious," she said. "Twins!" she called to the other side of the fence. "There are cookies!" Timidly the two Barnabys came through the gate and approached the porch. "How do you do and thank you for the ginger cookie," Nanny said, extending her hand, which the commander shook. "I am sorry to hear that you almost died of grief. Have you recovered?"

"I'm somewhat better," he replied. He passed the box of cookies around to the children. "My source of solace has been this lovely infant." He walked toward the end of the large porch, where a grinning baby with curly hair stood grasping the side of her playpen, and they followed him.

"It's not the same baby," Jane whispered to Tim. "Its hair isn't stubbly."

"It grew, dolt, since Mother chopped it off." Tim

looked nervously toward Nanny to see if she had heard the word *dolt,* which she had so recently forbidden. But she was leaning over the baby, smiling and talking in a babylike voice.

"What's your daughter's name, Commander?" she asked. "Oh, I see: *Ruth*. Sweet monogram."

"Yes, her name is Ruth. But she is not my daughter. She's my, ah, *ward*."

"Oh, lovely!" said Nanny. "You are an old-fashioned family, like us. We are four worthy orphans with a no-nonsense nanny."

"Like Mary Poppins?" suggested the man, with a pleased look of recognition.

"Not *one bit* like that fly-by-night woman," Nanny said with a sniff. "It almost gives me diabetes just to think of her: all those disgusting spoonfuls of sugar! None of that for me. I am simply a competent and professional nanny. And you are a—let me think—"

"Bereaved benefactor?" suggested the commander.

"Exactly. A bereaved benefactor with a ward. Like the uncle in *The Secret Garden*. What was his name? Oh yes: Archibald Craven."

"Oh my, no, not *one bit* like that ill-tempered scoundrel of an uncle. I am simply a well-to-do widower who happened to find a baby on my doorstep."

"We are both wonderfully old-fashioned, aren't we? Hello, Baby Ruth!" Nanny turned back to the baby and said in a sweet, high-pitched voice, "Aren't you fortunate to have found—" She hesitated. "What does she call you?" she asked the man.

"She doesn't speak yet. But I've been a bit worried about the question of what she will call me. I do like the sound of Papa," he said, and then paused and dabbed his eyes with his handkerchief. "But—"

"Brings back sad memories?" Nanny asked sympathetically.

"Indeed."

"Well, there is time. Children?" She turned to the four Willoughbys. "This is Baby Ruth."

They nodded awkwardly.

"Give her a gingersnap," she directed them. "They're not too spicy, are they, Commander? An infant this age shouldn't have spicy food."

"No," he said, "they're quite bland. She likes them. But thank you for alerting me to that. I am new to this and sometimes it is hard to know what is proper. I've been thinking, actually, about looking for a nanny. I don't suppose . . . " He gave her a questioning look.

"She's *ours,*" said Barnaby A, in an outraged tone.

"And we're orphans, or at least almost orphans, so we *need* her!"

"We must go now," said his twin. "It's almost time for dinner."

"We haven't even had lunch yet, B," Nanny pointed out.

"I meant the cat's dinner. It's almost time for our cat's dinner."

The children moved toward the porch steps. "Well," said Nanny to the commander, "it was lovely to meet you, but the children seem eager to move on. Perhaps our paths will cross again. Goodbye to you, Commander Melanoff.

"And bye-bye to you as well, Baby Ruth," she said to the infant, who waved back with a chubby hand.

"Wait! I don't know your names," Commander Melanoff said suddenly, just as Nanny was latching the gate behind her. The children were halfway down the street.

"I'm just Nanny," she called back. "The children are Tim, A, B, and Jane."

"A and B? How odd."

"They're twins," Nanny explained.

"I see," he replied, though he didn't.

"They are all Willoughbys."

He nodded. "Goodbye, then," he called. He turned to the playpen and to Ruth because it was time to take her inside for her afternoon nap. But he had a puzzled look on his face. *Willoughby,* he thought. There was something vaguely familiar about the name.

# 15.
## A REGRETTABLE TRANSACTION

"Uh-oh," Barnaby A said as they approached their own house at the end of their outing. "What's that on the sign?"

They had all become very accustomed to the FOR SALE CHEAP sign that was still tacked to their window box and to the tacked-on addition that announced the reduction of the price. And they were so accustomed to scurrying into their disguises and poses at the approach of prospective buyers that Jane could become a lamp in very few seconds and Tim could burrow under his fur rug in no time at all. Nanny took a little longer to transform herself into a statue of Aphrodite because, of course, she had to shed her clothes and powder herself and wrap herself in a sheet—all a little time consuming. But it was routine by now. The real estate agent would call to announce a showing of the house, and all of them would automatically move into their places, waiting for the sound of her key in the front-door lock.

Usually the showings were very short. Sometimes the prospective buyers never even reached the upstairs. That was always a bit of a disappointment to Nanny, and she was thinking of moving her statue's position perhaps to the parlor, where people would have a better view of Aphrodite.

*"Curses!"* Tim said in horror as he ran forward and read aloud the further addition to the sign. "Look at this! How could this have happened? We've been sold!"

"Oh, no!" Barnaby B groaned. "We should never have gone for a walk!"

"Terrible things always happen when one is out for a walk," Jane pointed out sadly. "Remember Little Red Riding Hood? And, oh dear, Hansel and Gretel?"

Nanny opened the door and hurried inside. On the hall table she found a hastily written note. "It's from the real estate agent," she explained with a worried look, and read it aloud to the children, who had gathered around her.

"'Congratulations! I'm sorry you weren't home when I called to announce our visit. But the house looked lovely and smelled so appealing—raisin cookies, I think—and the prospective buyer fell in love with it and has given me a ton of money. You have two weeks to leave. Please feel free to take your undies. Good luck.'"

"Oh, no!" the twins wailed.

"Drat!" said Tim with a scowl.

Jane stamped her foot and began to cry.

"Let us not waste time with tears and useless expostulations," Nanny told them. "What if this were a story in a book with a well-worn maroon leather binding? What would good old-fashioned people do in this situation?"

"They would call the sheriff," Tim said.

"Murder the villain," the twins suggested.

Jane simply continued to sob, and Nanny handed her a lace-trimmed hanky.

"They would make a plan," Nanny announced. "But first," she added, heading toward the kitchen and reaching for her apron where it hung on a wall hook, "they would bake a lemon soufflé." She opened the refrigerator and took out some eggs.

While the soufflé was in the oven—and during that time they all were required to tiptoe (because heavy footsteps can ruin a baking soufflé; not many people know this, Nanny pointed out, and that is why there are so many ruined soufflés in the world)—the mail was delivered in a whoosh through the mail slot of the front door.

"No-o-o!" wailed Tim, holding up a postcard. "They've again survived!"

Everyone tiptoed to his side, even Nanny, though she checked the oven time first (because a soufflé must be very carefully timed, she had told them, and not many people were careful enough about this aspect of soufflé baking). Tim read the card aloud.

"'Dear Ones—'"

"Hah!" they all said aloud, but quietly because of the soufflé (excessive noise can be the death of a soufflé, Nanny had explained).

"'Such an adventure! The helicopter crashed and the pilot plummeted into the raging volcano! Cleverly, we clung to a rotor and were spun to safe ground. Only the pilot was lost and it didn't matter because he was Presbyterian.

"'We wonder why the house is still unsold. Perhaps it is because of the cat. Please have her put to sleep.'"

Jane looked down at the cat, who had just rubbed against her legs with a loud purr. "She sleeps every night, and a lot during the day as well," she said. "Why should we put her to sleep more often? When would she pounce about chasing bits of fluff?"

Her brothers looked meaningfully at each other, wondering whether to explain to Jane what their parents had meant. Nanny shook her head at them. So they remained silent.

"Does it say anything else? Or just end with that cruel sentence about the cat?" Barnaby A asked.

"A bit more." Tim continued reading.

"'Now off to our next excursion! And this one on our own! No more guides for us! We are to climb an alp! One that has never been successfully climbed! It is cluttered with frozen bodies. But we are prepared. We have bought pitons for our feet and crampons to attach to our heads.'"

"I don't think pitons are for your feet," Barnaby B said. "I read a book about mountain climbing. Pitons are spikes that you hammer into the ice."

"I read the same book as B," said his twin. "Crampons are for your feet. For your boots, actually.

Why would they put them on their heads?"

"Because they are dolts," Tim said, remembering again that Nanny had outlawed the word and looking at her defiantly.

"They are dolts indeed," Nanny said. She stared at the postcard and murmured, "I myself am Presbyterian."

Jane was on her knees, playing with the cat. "Where are we going to live?" she asked piteously. "And can the cat come?"

The kitchen timer buzzed, and they tiptoed to the kitchen to eat soufflé and make a plan.

# 16.
## TWO TERRIBLE TOURISTS

The small Swiss village was so remote that travelers rarely passed through. Even the train that had been buried there six years before had been on its way to someplace else, to a different town with museums and shops that sold plastic models of alpenhorns and Saint Bernards.

For that reason, because it was such an unusual happening, the villagers took notice of the two tourists who arrived wearing sunglasses and carrying badly folded maps. The townspeople murmured to each other about the odd clothing: Bermuda shorts on both man and woman, and Birkenstock sandals on their feet. "Whatever are they doing here?" they said to each other in low voices. They watched the couple enter the small *gasthaus* on the main street.

"We need a big lunch," the man said to the waitress. He picked up the menu and glanced at it. "I can't read this. It isn't in English. Tell me, in a civilized language, what you have to eat. We need nourishment.

"We're going to climb that alp," the man announced loudly, pointing through the window toward the towering mountain.

His wife, looking at the guidebook, said, "Listen to this!" and read aloud to the pretty waitress, who was the daughter of the proprietor, "'Never been successfully climbed. With good binoculars one can see, in summer when the deepest snow has abated, the frozen bodies of several famous climbers. It is too dangerous for rescuers to retrieve these poor lost souls and they remain there as a reminder to others and a tribute to the ferocious power of this mountain.'" She pushed her sunglasses to the top of her head and squinted through the window.

"I can't see the bodies," she whined. "I want to see the frozen bodies."

"Can I get a good thick steak?" the man asked the waitress.

She shook her head, and he gave a sigh of exasperation. "These foreigners," he muttered irritably to his wife.

"Well, how about a Reuben sandwich?" he asked.

"No, I'm sorry," she said politely. "We have fondue. We're very proud of it. It is our national dish."

"*Fondue?* Good lord, do you know what I call that? Fon doo-doo, that's what. Well, we'll have hamburgers. We need something substantial. And some drinks with *ice cubes* in them, for heaven's sake. I don't know why, in a country with ice everywhere, one can't get a drink with ice cubes."

The pretty waitress took a deep breath. "I'm sorry. No hamburgers. I could ask Father to make you a cheese sandwich."

Grouchily they agreed to cheese sandwiches and grouchily they ate them when they arrived. Then they grouchily paid the bill without leaving a tip.

"What are you staring at?" the man asked the waitress as they turned to leave.

She blushed, and apologized. She had been staring, actually, at their heads, thinking for a moment that they may be royalty because they seemed to be wearing crowns of some sort and because they had *acted* a bit like titled people from minor principalities. Now, however, she could see that on their heads they were wearing hiking equipment intended, actually, for the soles of hiking boots. It was quite startling.

Later, when the two had gone, headed to the trail at the foot of the mountain, noisily dragging the pitons that they had attached by string to their ankles, the waitress cleared the table and said in a worried voice to her father, "They're planning to climb the mountain. But they don't even have warm clothing. And for some reason they are wearing crampons on their heads."

He shrugged.

"Should we send someone out to stop them?"

"We Swiss never get involved," he said. "Anyway, no one is available. Everyone is going to the wedding. So are we." He went to the door of the *gasthaus* and hung a sign there that said GESCHLOSSEN, BIN AUF HOCHZEIT: *Closed for a wedding.*

The wedding was a very exciting event for the village. Finally, after years of bachelorhood—so many that his mother had been wringing her hands in despair—the tall, thin postmaster, Hans-Peter, had fallen wildly and wonderfully in love with the somewhat mysterious and very meticulous foreign lady who had been rescued from the avalanche. She had already rearranged his postal boxes as well as his kitchen utensils. On this day they were being married in the village church at the foot of the forbidding mountain. The bride was wearing an edelweiss wreath in her neatly curled hair. Her young son, in his lederhosen, was acting as ring bearer.

Not only the post office but all of the local shops were closed for the afternoon. All of the villagers gathered, first for the ceremony and then for the lengthy celebration, which included yodeling, beer drinking, and many dances in which the dancers bumped their behinds together and clapped their hands.

A happy day, to be sure.

But not for the bride's son. For his mother's sake, he danced and yodeled and smiled. He was polite to the postmaster and called him Schtepfader. But beneath his pretense, the boy was deeply unhappy not just at the wedding, but in the little village. Nothing about Switzerland agreed with him. He was very clumsy on skis. The sound of cowbells hurt his ears. He was allergic to cheese, and cuckoo clocks made him very nervous. He had twice nicked his fingers with his Swiss army knife. His lederhosen itched, and his knees were always cold. And though the memories were blurred after such a long time, and though his mother had said again and again, "If he cared about us he would have written!" the boy did recall a kind and loving man with a thick mustache, a man he had called Papa, who had once read to him, animal or adventure stories usually, in a quiet voice while they sat together in a porch swing.

He wanted desperately to go home.

# 17.
## AN AUSPICIOUS CHANGE

It was surprising to the Willoughby children—and to Nanny—how difficult it was to plan their own futures, now that they were parentless and soon to be homeless as well.

"I think this would be easier if we were modern children," Tim said, "but we are old-fashioned. So our choices are limited. Jane?"

"Yes?" Jane asked. She was on the floor, playing with the cat again.

"I think you must develop a lingering disease and waste away, eventually dying a slow and painless death. We will all gather around your deathbed and you can murmur your last words. Like Beth in *Little Women*."

Jane scowled. "I don't want to," she said.

Tim ignored that. "Nanny?"

She was at the sink, rinsing the plates on which she had served the soufflé. She turned, wiped her hands on her apron, and looked at Tim curiously. "Yes?"

"You must renounce the world and enter a cloistered convent. We will visit once a year and talk to you through a grill. All but Jane, of course, because she'll be tragically dead, cut off in the flower of her youth."

"I *told* you. I'm Presbyterian. We don't enter convents."

Tim thought. "Missionary work, then. Prepare to go to darkest Africa and convert heathens."

Nanny scowled and picked up a dishtowel.

"What about us?" the twins asked together.

"A and B: you must run away and join the circus. Toby Tyler did that. Remember we read that book?"

"Yes," said Barnaby A. "I liked it. It was very old-fashioned. Toby was an orphan, very worthy—"

"—and his pet monkey died," finished Barnaby B.

"But we don't *like* the circus," Barnaby A said, "except for occasional elephants."

"And we're allergic to hay," his brother pointed out.

"Old-fashioned children do not have allergies," Tim announced. "If you don't like the running-away-to-the-circus idea, then you can build a raft and sail down the Mississippi like Huckleberry Finn."

"We can't swim!" the twins wailed.

"That makes it even more of an old-fashioned adventure. Now, as for me—"

"Yes, what about you? We're all off dying of obsolete diseases and sneezing with allergies and drowning in whirlpools and getting lost in the jungle looking for heathens, and you're probably planning something wonderful for yourself!" Barnaby A said angrily.

"Not a bit. I'm going to have a typical old-fashioned-boy future. First of all, I'm going to pull myself up by my bootstraps, and—"

"What are bootstraps, exactly?" asked Jane, looking up from the floor, where she was tantalizing the cat with a piece of straw from the broom.

"Never mind. It's not important. I'm going to wear torn, patched clothing and sell newspapers on cold, windy street corners, saving every hard-won penny, in hopes that someday a well-to-do businessman, maybe with a beautiful daughter, will recognize my worthiness, like Ragged Dick in that book by what-was-his-name, Horatio Alger? Remember him? And—"

"A well-to-do businessman," repeated Nanny. "You mean a tycoon?"

"Yes, exactly. A wealthy industrialist."

"A benefactor?"

"Pollyanna had a benefactor!" Jane recalled. "Not till the end of the book, though."

"Yes," said Tim. "This will be like that. And he will—"

"I have an idea," Nanny said suddenly, untying her apron.

Tim scowled. "You're always interrupting, Nanny! And what do you mean, you have an idea? I've had a whole *list* of them!" he said.

"But we don't *like* your ideas," said Jane. She stood up; the cat, startled, scurried out of the kitchen, pretending that it had planned all along to leave. "What's your idea, Nanny?"

But Nanny had left the kitchen as well. She had retrieved her official dark blue nanny cape from the closet in the hall, had flung it around herself, and was opening the front door. "I'll be back in an hour, children," she called.

* * *

And so it happened that the entire Willoughby family, plus Nanny, and the cat, moved into the mansion. When Nanny, reminded of him by the mention of benefactors and tycoons, had described their plight to Commander Melanoff and volunteered to take on the role of caregiver for Baby Ruth, his eyes lit up with joy. A few days later, they pulled the wagon, containing packed boxes of undies and the cat in its carrier, to their new home, leaving everything else behind except what they were wearing, which included the beige sweater (it was Barnaby A's day for the sweater), because Commander Melanoff assured them that he would provide for all their needs.

They threw themselves on his mercy, as old-fashioned people tend to do. "We have no money," Tim explained nervously. "The real estate lady said that the buyer paid tons of money for our house. But she isn't giving us any. She's mailing it to our parents."

"And they are off climbing an alp," Jane added.

"Oh, please," Commander Melanoff said, clutching his handkerchief and dabbing at his eyes, "don't mention that word, if you don't mind."

*"Climbing?"* asked Jane, her eyes wide.

"No, the *A* word. It brings back sad memories. We'll change the subject. And we won't discuss money again. No need. I have oodles."

"However did you get oodles of money?" asked Tim with interest. "I'd like to do that someday. I've thought about standing on cold, windy street corners, selling—"

"No, no. You have to invent something. And you have to give it a wonderful name. I myself invented a kind of candy years ago—a long black spiral flavored with anise—and I named it Lickety Twist. It made me a billionaire."

"You invented Lickety Twist? We *love* Lickety Twist!" the twins exclaimed.

"Nanny won't let us have it, though," Jane pointed out.

"No, we have to sneak it. She says it's bad for our teeth." Barnaby A opened his mouth wide. "I have a cavity," he said. "See?"

"Oh, it's terrible for your teeth," Commander Melanoff agreed. "I never eat it myself, and when Ruth is old enough to chew well, I'll see that she has only apples and an occasional ginger cookie. *Never* will she have Lickety Twist."

"But what about all the poor children who do eat it and rot their teeth?" Jane asked sadly.

The commander sighed. "Ah," he said, "that is how we billionaires exist, I am sad to say. *Caveat emptor.* We profit on the misfortune of others."

"But you do good," Jane reassured him sweetly, patting his hand. "You adopt babies."

"And you also take in needy children," said Barnaby A.

"And hire homeless nannies," added Barnaby B.

"I do like Nanny," the commander said, his face brightening. "She's a handsome, competent woman. She takes my mind off my sorrows. Where is she, by the way?" He looked around.

"Tending Ruth and making dinner," Tim told him. "A minute ago she did the laundry and scrubbed the bathtubs."

"What a wonder she is," murmured the commander.

"She plans to wax the floors later."

"An absolute wonder. Does she, ah, have a husb— well, what I mean is, is she a married woman?"

"Oh, no, she's an old-fashioned person. A spinster of little means," Tim explained. "Well educated and of good reputation, but forced to go into domestic service because her father died in debt and left her penniless."

Commander Melanoff sighed. "A familiar story. Like Jane Eyre. Well," he said, "let us hope that like most old-fashioned stories, this one will have a happy ending."

# 18.
## A Walking Tour Is
## Suggested

"You're getting thin, dear," the postmaster's new wife commented one morning to her boy. "Have some more cream on your muesli."

"I'm sorry, Mother, but I despise muesli," he said.

"*Deutsch*, please," the postmaster told him. He wanted very much for the boy's German to improve. He thought he might like the boy better if his German were better.

"Mein muesli ist dischgusting." The boy poked his spoon into the bowl lethargically. "It makesch me vant to womit."

"He eats practically nothing," his mother told her husband.

"He is lacking in self-discipline. Does he do his knee bends each morning along with his deep-breathing exercises? Does he read a chapter of the Bible every day? Does he pick up his toys?"

"No. He spends hours arranging his little army men in battle positions on his toy table and then at bedtime he leaves them there. I've told him again and again that they must be put away in their boxes every evening, but he pays no attention. And his room is untidy. I've organized his clothing alphabetically, but then I go in and I find that he has hung his shirts next to his pajamas though I have repeatedly told him that shirts belong beside shorts and shoes. And the corners of his bed are not tucked in properly."

The postmaster shook his head and looked at the boy with disappointment. Then he looked at his watch. "I am almost two minutes behind schedule," he announced, and folded his napkin carefully into thirds.

His new wife smiled at him. "Lunch will be at twelve twenty-seven p.m.," she said.

"Good," he replied, precisely adjusting the lapels of his uniform jacket and removing a piece of lint from his sleeve. He leaned over and kissed her on her forehead. "You have a hair out of place, beloved one," he told her affectionately. "There, on the top."

"I'll rebraid," she promised him.

"Perhaps," he added as he was going through the door, "the boy would benefit from a walking tour? A few weeks of hiking might toughen him up."

After his stepfather was gone, the boy looked up from his uneaten museli. "Did he mean I would go all alone?" he asked his mother.

"Yes, dear. It's the way that old-fashioned boys become robust and mature. Especially ones who have become wasted and weak, like you, and pathetic and disorganized."

"Would you give me a map?"

"Oh, yes. And some vitamins and cough drops in your backpack."

"But I would be on my own?"

"Don't be frightened, dear. Many old-fashioned boys have done it, and most have survived."

"Could I choose my own route, or would you plan it all out for me in your meticulous way?"

His mother sighed. "I would *like* to do that, dear. But it is customary for the solitary hiker to find his own way. You would be following your dream. It would be your quest." She hummed a few bars of "Dream the Impossible Dream" and went to wind the cuckoo clock that hung on the kitchen wall.

Without noticing the dry, medicinal taste of the muesli, the boy began to eat his breakfast in hurried gulps. He was thinking now of his own quest, his own dreams, his vague memories of his papa. "How soon could I leave?" he asked.

His mother finished winding the clock, and checked the time against her own Swiss watch. "In about an hour?" she suggested. It was time now, the time immediately after breakfast, for his knee bends and Bible reading. But her son ignored those things. Excitedly he went to his room to pack.

By the time that Hans-Peter, the postmaster, came home for his 12:27 p.m. lunch, the boy was gone. His room was empty. The postmaster's wife had packed away the toy soldiers, stored the clothing in alphabetized, labeled boxes, and repainted the walls.

# 19.
## LONG HOURS IN THE LABORATORY

Commander Melanoff, whose life was greatly changed now that he had Nanny to tend Ruth, began to spend hours each day in the experimental laboratory in one of the mansion's turrets. He had always been happiest in the lab, where he could mix and measure and taste things in his ongoing search for the next hugely successful candy, the thing that would rival Lickety Twist and add more billions to his fortune.

He had to admit, privately, that it was easier to do his experiments with his wife still buried in the avalanche and now, clearly, long (he sniffed at the thought) dead.

She had insisted on tidying the lab all the time. Every time he thought he had come *close,* had been *very near* to the kind of perfection he sought—just the right combination of nuts and chocolate and caramel and marshmallow and raisins—he would return eagerly the next morning and find it all gone: the containers washed and dried and put away (bowls to the left of cartons, pans before pots, stirring spoons arranged by size) and his scribbled notes about proportions taken out with the trash. With a sigh, he would begin again: measuring, stirring, simmering, tasting. But his efforts had seemed doomed.

And then, of course, with the avalanche tragedy, he had lost his enthusiasm and the utensils in the lab had gathered dust for years. Now, with renewed vigor, he washed everything, unpacked new ingredients, and began again.

Carefully he melted and measured some chocolate.

Through the closed door of the lab, he could hear the cheerful, busy sounds of the household: the children playing, Nanny scrubbing and cooking, Baby Ruth giggling in her playpen, the cats (for the Willoughby cat had made friends quite quickly with the Melanoff cat) leaping about and pouncing on imaginary mice.

Happily he chopped some nuts. He added them to the chocolate, dipped a finger in for a taste, thought it over, and decided that it had been a mistake. He remembered now that the chocolate should coat the *outside* of the candy bar; the nuts should be mixed with the caramel on the *inside*. He threw away the chocolate-and-nuts mixture and began again.

Below, downstairs, he heard the oven timer in the kitchen make its buzzing signal. He could picture Nanny, in her flowered apron, leaning down and opening the oven door to peer inside at whatever fine-smelling thing she was cooking for dinner. Oh, if he were not such a *decent* man, he might be tempted to pat her large behind affectionately as she bent over.

Shaking his head to rid it of such improper thoughts, he stirred the freshly melted chocolate and set it aside. In another pan he began to warm and soften some caramel. Again he picked up his chopping knife and went to work on some walnuts. When they were reduced to small bits, he sprinkled them into the warm caramel, dipped in his finger, and tasted. *No,* he thought. They should be *pecans,* not walnuts. He sighed, but it was not a sigh of frustration; it was more a little breath of happiness and creativity (combined, slightly, with the thought of Nanny, below in the kitchen), and he began again.

Of course, he thought, although the perfect combination of ingredients was essential, still (as he had explained to the children) he would need the perfect name for this new confection. He would have it printed in blue, he thought. No: *red*. He would have it printed in large red letters on the wrapper of the candy bar.

*Choco-nut? Pecan-o-choc?* Silly names. He dismissed them in his mind and began chopping pecans. The name didn't need to contain the ingredients, he realized. His previous success had started with a mention of the act of eating—*lick* had become Lickety-Twist. This candy bar, with all its caramel, would involve chewing. *Chew,* he thought. *Chewy-Gooey.* That had a ring to it.

He pictured in his mind a child at a candy counter. "I want a Chewy-Gooey."

"I want *three* Chewy-Gooeys." He could imagine the eagerness with which buyers would place their orders.

He frowned and poured the chopped pecans into the fresh pan of melted caramel. Maybe it wasn't really a good idea to refer to gooey-ness. It might make parents nervous. They would think about cavities and dental bills.

From below, he could hear happy laughter and Nanny's cheerful singsong voice: "Patty-cake, patty-cake! Baker's man!" He pictured her softly clapping her hands, and he imagined the infant's delighted smile. Sweet child. Baby Ruth.

# 20.
## A CONFECTIONARY
## RECOGNITION

The boy had hiked happily to the next village, yodeling a bit as he walked the path, waving now and then to milkmaids and shepherds, picking an occasional flower. Here in the open hills he found that the sound of the cowbells, which had previously caused his head to ache, was now a charming background to the scenery: the blue sky, the green blossom-strewn meadows, the snowy Alps. He glanced upward at the towering peak whose shadow fell across his own village and thought with a surge of pride of those brave climbers who had been lost on its heights. He had peered through a neighbor's binoculars once and seen them there, frozen forever, dotting the sheer icy cliffs. There was talk of putting their outlines on a postage stamp or perhaps even the Swiss flag. National heroes, they were, those stiff shapes with their ropes and axes. One had been there for more than fifty years.

Though the boy could not see this from where he walked, two more figures had now joined that illustrious group. Quick-frozen as Popsicles, crampons on their heads like crowns, their Birkenstocks and Bermuda shorts stiffened into museum-quality artifacts in the clear, thin air, Mr. and Mrs. Willoughby had become the late Mr. and Mrs. Willoughby, and their children were true orphans— and heirs—at last.

The boy, trudging along and thinking about an itinerary, a plan for his quest, regretted that he had not paid more careful attention to the letters that his mother, with increasing annoyance, sent off to his father, the letters that were never answered. He knew the name Melanoff, of course; it was his own name. But he had no idea where to look for, or how to find, the man he had once called Papa.

Entering the next small village, with its red-shuttered wooden houses, each decorated with window boxes filled with geraniums and marigolds, the boy looked around for a shop. He was hungry. Although his mother had not packed food for him—his knapsack was filled with clean underwear and vitamins—he had, at the last minute, remembered to bring money. He had opened his bank with its small gold key and removed his savings: quite a significant amount. His mother was a wealthy woman and there had been no way to shop or spend during the years they had lived in the buried train car. Dutifully she had given him his substantial allowance every week. When they were rescued, she had taken her own money to the local bank because she was a sensible and organized woman. But the boy had not wanted to part with his. He liked the crisp bills with their interesting pictures; he was especially fond of the hundred-franc note that showed a blond boy feeding a lamb. And so, although his mother pointed out that he would not be earning interest, she allowed him to keep his savings at home.

Now the bills filled the pockets of his lederhosen and the crevices within his knapsack, and his hat, with its silly feather that he loathed, was stuffed with Swiss francs as well.

In the small shop and café next to the little train station, he bought a meat salad called *Wurstsalat*; *Apfelküchlein,* a deep-fried apple cookie that he loved; and a glass of milk. From the café he watched a train enter the station, discharge two passengers, and continue on, disappearing around the mountains. His hunger was satisfied and he felt happy, but he was beginning to worry a bit about his own lack of a plan. Perhaps the village had an inn where he could spend the night? Or, as a good old-fashioned boy might, in order to save money, he could curl up in a barn?

But a boy with a quest, he knew, should be getting on with it, should be pursuing his dream, not lolling about in a barn, daydreaming. Thinking, considering his options, the boy decided to finish his lunch with a piece of candy, something he had never been allowed at home. It felt grown up and a bit dangerous, buying candy. But there was a selection in the small shop's glass case. Mostly Swiss chocolates. He examined them, leaning forward against the glass, trying to choose among the exotic names that were lettered on small cards: *Mandoline, Giandujotti, Stracciatella, Noisettine, Nussfin, Caramelita, Amande de Luxe, Nussor, Macchiato, Cornet Reve,* and *Noccino.*

The shopkeeper watched the boy with an amused smile. These elegant chocolates were most often purchased by travelers wanting to take a gift home. He gestured to the boy, indicating a different selection, the ordinary, everyday candies that children of the village bought with their coins. He watched the boy's eyes light up as if he had recognized an old friend.

"Oh! I'll take *that!*" he said enthusiastically to the shopkeeper, pointing. Then he remembered to speak German. "Vat callen zei it?"

The shopkeeper reached into the case and handed the long spiral candy to the boy. "Lickety Twist," he said.

Memories flooded back. In his best German the boy asked if he could see the original wrapper in which the candy had been packed. The shopkeeper, being Swiss, was too polite to criticize the terrible German and so orderly that he had folded the discarded wrapping neatly and put it away. Now he retrieved it and handed it to the boy, who examined it with a surge of excitement. The wrapping contained the address of the Melanoff candy factory.

It was a very long distance—halfway around the world—from the small Swiss village. The boy looked around, thinking about the magnitude of such a journey. From where he stood, he could hear a rooster in a nearby farmyard, children singing in a kindergarten, and the rush of water from a small waterfall that tumbled down from the rocks at the foot of the mountain. Everything here in Switzerland was placid and beautiful and had not changed, it seemed, in a hundred, perhaps a thousand, years.

One of his scratchy wool knee socks was prickered with twigs and had drooped on his leg. He glanced down at it, thinking how distressed his mother would have been to see that he looked disheveled. He grinned. Then, sucking his long, pliable candy, the boy went next door to the little railroad station and studied the maps attached to the wall for a few long, silent minutes. Finally, with a feeling of adventure and a determined sense of future, he bought a ticket to Rotterdam.

## 21.

## A DECISION, AN ANNOUNCMENT, AND
## AN UNEXPECTED ARRIVAL

It had taken a month. But Commander Melanoff felt certain, taking a test bite alone in his lab, that the candy was perfect. His masterpiece. So many false starts! He chuckled now, realizing that it had been simple in the end: the addition of a tiny portion of nougat before he poured the melted chocolate over and allowed it to harden on the small, delectable bar.

Now that his experimental work was complete, he would give the formula, the recipe, to the workers at his factory, and they could begin production, mixing the ingredients in huge stainless-steel vats. Thousands of the bars would soon be popping out in orderly rows from the final machine, and then they would go to the packaging department, where they would be hygienically sealed into their paper wrappers with the name in bright red letters, then packed into cartons and shipped to distributors throughout the world.

Soon they would appear in corner stores, in movie theater refreshment cases, in vending machines everywhere. He could picture them there. He could picture laughing children, indulgent grandmothers, teenagers, all of them, pointing to what would soon be familiar red letters and asking for—

Asking for—

He groaned. The name! He still wasn't certain what the name should be.

But he had begun to feel that it should not be a name referring to any ingredients or to any body mechanics: no licking or chewing or munching references. No. It needed something unusual—something *sweet*—as a name.

He was actually thinking about naming the new candy bar after his child.

Downstairs in the mansion, Baby Ruth was playing, as she often did, in the front hall. She had just learned to walk. Still unsteady on her chubby legs, she toddled across the Oriental rug, trying to catch the cats, who twitched their tails mischievously to tease her but were adept at leaping just out of her reach as she approached.

The twins were playing a game of checkers in the parlor, and Tim was industriously putting together a model airplane out of balsa wood, being very careful not to sniff the glue. In the kitchen Jane was helping Nanny frost some cupcakes.

Commander Melanoff came down from the laboratory to announce the final perfection of the candy he'd been working on now for a month. He had a proud look, thinking of his candy; and when he stood on the lowest landing of the elegant staircase and saw his family busy with their happy enterprises, his look became fond, as well. Such a short time ago he had been a grieving, miserable, and messy— yes, he had to admit, *messy*—man who thought there was nothing left to look forward to. Now there were delicious odors wafting in from the kitchen. There were five children in residence who were old-fashioned, well behaved, clean, healthy, and bright. Twilight streamed in through the high windows, and the windows were clean and well polished. The floors gleamed with wax.

Commander Melanoff looked around and smiled with pride and satisfaction. The only thing within his sight that was slightly jarring—a little off-putting, a wee bit out of order—was the huge stack of crumpled and yellowing papers against the wall. It had been there so long that the cats no longer batted at it, and Baby Ruth had outgrown her interest in it now that she could walk and had other things to examine.

But the commander noticed it now, and thought briefly about what it represented of his sad past. He considered what he should do. Then he cleared his throat loudly, as if preparing to make an announcement.

Everyone looked up, even the cats.

Nanny emerged from the kitchen with a spatula in one hand and Jane by her side.

"I've made a decision," Commander Melanoff announced.

"You've chosen a name for the candy?" asked Tim.

The commander shook his head. "Oh, *that*. Yes, I think so. But that is not the topic of my decision."

Barnaby A surreptitiously made his move on the checkerboard, took one of his brother's men, and kinged himself.

"Dinner's almost ready. Chicken," Nanny pointed out. "Not to rush you."

"I'll be brief," the commander replied. "Gather round, everyone. Nanny. Baby Ruth. Willoughbys: Tim, A, B, and Jane." (He had become accustomed to the names A and B, but he thought again, as he often had, that there was something puzzlingly *familiar* about the name Willoughby.)

He smiled at all of them from the stairs when they had gathered curiously to hear his announcement.

"This house," he began, "has changed greatly in the past months. All because of you. Each one of you.

"Baby Ruth, of course, who appeared so mysteriously and soothed my grief." The toddler, recognizing her name, grinned and giggled. "One day, quite soon, a fabulous candy bar will be named for her.

"Tim." The commander looked at the boy fondly. "What can I say about a fine old-fashioned lad? Of course we all lament the regrettable and mysterious loss of your parents. But in the true spirit of orphanhood you have pulled yourself up by your bootstraps, and—"

"What *are* bootstraps, exactly?" whispered Jane loudly.

"Shhh," Tim told her.

The commander continued. "—and one day in the future, I will send you to law school and you shall become 'of counsel' to Melanoff Industries."

"A and B?" Commander Melanoff looked benignly at the twins. It was a Tuesday, and Barnaby B was wearing the sweater. The overlong sleeves had made it difficult to move his checkers on the board. But the twins were accustomed to that obstacle. Tomorrow Barnaby A would wear the sweater and the handicap would be reversed.

"What can I say about these lovely boys? They remind me of—" He sniffed and wiped his eyes. "They are the age that—" He dabbed again with his hanky. "Well. I won't dwell on my own tragedy. I will only say that one day, when you come of age, I will select names for you so that you will no longer be labeled inadequately by letters. I will—"

"We *have* names," the twins said, in unison.

"Shhh," Tim told them.

"And dear Jane," the commander went on. "Such an adorable, self-assured little girl, who—"

"I'm hungry," Jane said loudly.

"Shhh," Tim told her.

The commander blew Jane a kiss.

"Finally, dear Nanny." Commander Melanoff fixed his eyes on Nanny with a lovesick gaze. "She has made my house a home. Once it was filthy; now it is clean. Once it was cold; now it is warm. Once it was quiet; now it rejoices. Once—"

"Commander," said Nanny in her no-nonsense voice, "it's not just chicken. It is chicken breasts cooked in a lemon-and-caper sauce, and it is congealing and will soon be inedible. Could we hurry this speech along?"

The commander chuckled. "I'm sorry. I do meander, conversationally. And all of this speechmaking was just preliminary to my announcement. We'll go and eat our dinner right away. The announcement was simply that I have decided to do away with The Stack!"

He gestured dramatically toward the immense pile of unopened letters and telegrams from Switzerland. "After dinner—is there dessert, by the way?"

Nanny nodded. "Crème caramel," she told him, "if it hasn't burned to a crisp."

"After dessert," he went on, "we will make a fire in the fireplace and we will *burn* The Stack, little by little."

"Shall we open everything first?" asked Tim. "It would take forever."

"No need," Commander Melanoff said. "It is simply repetitions of terrible news. I stopped opening them after the first year and a half. We will burn them unopened."

They began to move toward the dining room, where the table was set for dinner. Nanny picked up Baby Ruth and carried her to her mahogany highchair.

"He's right," Jane said sweetly from her seat as she unfolded her linen napkin and laid it tidily on the lap of her ruffled frock. "I opened a lot of them. They were very boring."

"Did you, dear?" Nanny placed the platter of chicken in front of Commander Melanoff. "Were you practicing your reading, like a good girl?"

Jane nodded. "Yes. But it was just 'when are you coming to get us, when are you coming to get us' over and over."

"Who was supposed to come get who?" Tim asked. He began to pass the plates, each with its serving of chicken, around.

"*Whom,* dear," Nanny reminded him.

Commander Melanoff drizzled some of the

lemon-and-caper sauce on his chicken. He tasted a bit and closed his eyes in delight. "Yummy, Nanny," he said. "As always."

"Who was supposed to come get whom, Jane?" Tim asked again, grammatically correct this time.

Jane shrugged. "I don't know. She never said. And then the next year, she was angry. The letters kept saying, 'I never liked you anyway, you old goat. You never picked up your dirty socks.'"

"*Old goat* is not a very pleasant phrase," Nanny told her. "Let's never use it ourselves."

"Would you pass me some of that broccoli, A?" Commander Melanoff said politely. "Help yourself first."

"She said worse than 'old goat,'" Jane pointed out.

"Who did, dear?" the commander asked. "Have you tried the broccoli? There's a smidgen of grated cheese on it, I think."

"I don't know who. She didn't ever say her name." Jane tasted the broccoli. "But that last letter, the one that came last month, the one you put on the very tippy-top of the stack? That one had a bad word in it."

Commander Melanoff sighed. "Those rescuers. It must have become so frustrating for them over the years. I should have told them to stop digging long ago. I'm sorry they used a bad word, Jane. Let's never think about it again."

"It wasn't a *they*," Jane told him. "It was a *she*. May I say the bad word?"

"Just once, and very softly." Nanny gave her permission.

A hush fell over the table as everyone waited for Jane, sweet Jane, to say a bad word. Jane scrunched up her face, remembering the letter exactly. Then she recited softly what she had read:

"'You old fart, your son is just like you; he never picks up after himself. My new husband and I have sent him off to make his own way in the world. Good riddance to you both.'"

Jane glanced at Nanny. "*Riddance* is a very bad word and I won't ever say it again."

But no one heard Jane. They heard only the crashing sound of Commander Melanoff's chair tipping over as he leaped to his feet, dashed to the hall, and began pawing through the stack of mail. They could hear him sobbing loudly and repeating the words "My son! My son!"

Next, still sitting there stunned by the turn of events, they heard the shrill ring of the doorbell.

Nanny rose abruptly and ran forward, and all of the children followed except Baby Ruth, who, confined to her highchair, banged her spoon happily and chortled when the two cats jumped onto the table and began eating the chicken.

"Tell whoever it is to go away," sobbed Commander Melanoff. He was kneeling on the floor surrounded by envelopes, which he was tearing open one by one as he wept. "I can't face anyone now."

Nanny opened the door politely, prepared to follow his instructions. But she stepped back, startled, at the sight of a young boy, shivering in the chilly evening. His hair was uncut, shaggy, and down to his shoulders. His face was dirty. He was thin and unkempt, wearing an odd pair of short leather pants that were ragged and grease stained. His exposed knees were scraped and bruised, and his woolen socks were torn and sagging.

"It's Peter the goat-herd," murmured Tim in astonishment, "right out of *Heidi*! We can teach him to read and write, and then we'll all smile and hug and say religious things!"

"Shhh," Nanny scolded him. She stood aside and allowed the bedraggled boy to enter. He looked around at each of them in turn with no sign of recognition. But his face changed when he caught sight of the heavy man in the tweed jacket who was kneeling and weeping on the hall floor. His eyes lit up.

"Papa!" he said. "I've come home!"

# EPILOGUE

Oh, what is there to say at the happy conclusion of an old-fashioned story?

There are details to be filled in and explained, of course, and reference made to future events.

How did Commander Melanoff's young son make his way halfway around the world, with only a silly feathered hat full of Swiss francs and no passport or other official documents? Well, he was an old-fashioned, enterprising lad. In Rotterdam, one of the major seaports of Europe, he stowed away on a vessel heading across the Atlantic with its cargo. He was discovered, of course, and put to work as a cabin boy: badly treated, overworked, never paid, and his clean underwear was stolen by brigands in the Azores. But he made it to his destination and was the better for it, having overcome hardships so successfully. He would go on eventually to become the president of his father's company and to maintain its reputation for the finest of confectionaries.

Sad to say, the candy bar that the commander had worked so hard on never became a success. Perhaps the fault lay in its name. He had often said—thinking of Lickety Twist, such a triumph!—that the name was everything. But he had named the candy bar Little Ruthie and it simply never caught on.

He didn't care, really. His fortune was already vast, and when his son was restored to him—and when he married Nanny (it should come as no surprise that that is what he did)—he felt fulfilled in every way.

Names, though, did remain a bit of a problem. In the happy confusion on the evening of Commander Melanoff's son's reappearance, one of the twins asked the disheveled boy, "What's your name?"

And the boy replied, "Barnaby."

The twins looked at each other. "C?" one suggested.

"See what?" asked the new Barnaby.

"See my son!" Commander Melanoff exclaimed, still beside himself with joy. He cupped the boy's dirty face in his hands, kissed each cheek, and beamed down at him.

"No," the twins explained. "We meant that we're also Barnabys."

"I'm Barnaby A," said one.

"And I'm Barnaby B. So he has to be C."

"Nonsense! No son of mine is going to be C! Do you two have middle names? We'll rename you with your middle names."

The twins sighed and shuffled their feet in embarrassment. Tim stepped forward to explain. "I'm Timothy Anthony Malachy Willoughby," he pointed out, "because our parents, who were—excuse me, Nanny—*dolts,* thought it was important to have as many syllables as possible. That is, if one was a boy." He glanced sympathetically at his sister, Jane.

"And so the twins are—?"

"Well, the night the twins were born, they had just been to an Italian restaurant. So they are—" He looked at his brothers. "Do you want to say it?" he asked them. The twins nodded.

"I'm Barnaby Linguini Rotini Willoughby," one said with a sigh.

"And I'm Barnaby Ravioli Fusilli Willoughby," his brother, blushing, explained.

"Oh my goodness," Commander Melanoff said. "I don't quite know what to do about that. But I am not fond of A, B, and C. I fear it will hinder you eventually in the business world.

"Any suggestions?" He looked around, seeking help.

"Why don't we change their names?" Tim said.

"Yes! I'd so like to be Bill!" Barnaby A said.

"And could I be Joe?" his twin asked.

And so it was done. They went before a judge, were adopted along with their sister and brother, and became Bill and Joe, which they remained their entire lives, very happily. After the children all became official Melanoffs, the commander stopped wondering where he had heard the name Willoughby before. (Had he not burned it along with all the Swiss correspondence, he might have reread the note that had once been attached to Baby Ruth, noticed the penciled instruction—"If there is any reward to be had for this beastly baby, it *must* go to the Willoughbys"—and it would have answered the question. But it might have raised new questions, and so it is fortuitous that the note—and the mystery—disappeared.)

The third Barnaby retained his name but was always known as Junior. (Commander Melanoff's name, it seemed, was *also* Barnaby.) He later invented something called Junior Mints, which might have been quite successful, had someone else, as it turned out, not already invented them. Nothing ever surpassed Lickety Twist.

Baby Ruth, when she became an adult, made a search for her biological mother and found that the woman's life had taken a turn for the better and she was now living quite comfortably in Champaign, Illinois. Ruth had the wicker basket gold-plated, as a souvenir, and gave it to her for Christmas.

She married, surprisingly, her stepbrother Tim, who, as predicted, became an attorney. The brass plate on his office door at the candy factory said: TIMOTHY ANTHONY MALACHY WILLOUGHBY MELANOFF, ESQUIRE, OF COUNSEL. The job allowed him to be bossy and belittling, but he adored his wife and was never ruthless again.

The twins, Bill and Joe, never married. Today they operate a chain of clothing stores called Big Sweaters, which offers two-for-one prices to parents of twins.

Jane grew up and became a professor of feminist literature. Eventually she married a man named Smith and had triplet daughters, whom she named Lavender, Arpeggio, and Noxzema.

The postmaster and his wife, in Switzerland, ran the little post office efficiently for many, many years. They never had children, and just as well, because they didn't care for the mess that children made. Sometimes Commander Melanoff, with his second wife, Nanny, and their six children when they were still young, visited Switzerland on vacations: hiking in the summer, skiing in the winter. They always cordially stopped in the village post office to say hello and have a cup of tea.

During such visits, the four former Willoughbys, who had no connection, after all, to the postmaster and his wife, always excused themselves politely and took a few moments to walk together up the serene little path nearby. There, at the foot of the mountain, they stood solemnly, passing binoculars back and forth and gazing at the treacherous peak that had orphaned the four of them. Together they saluted the distant figures of their parents, who had frozen into place, happy to have achieved such heights, with gleaming smiles on their faces forever.

It was not a sad occasion, really. Just something the Willoughbys did and always followed with cocoa.

## THE END

# GLOSSARY

**ACQUISITION** means something that you have just gotten or received. Libraries and museums actually have acquisition departments, which obtain new things for their collections. If your dad is a stockbroker or a lawyer, ask him what "mergers and acquisitions" means. Fifty points if you understand his answer.

**AFFABLE** means good-natured and friendly. There are whole groups of people who are known for being affable. Cheerleaders, for example. Or Mormon missionaries.

**ALABASTER** is actually a kind of mineral used for sculptures. But it can also be an adjective meaning white like that mineral. See if you can remember where the word *alabaster* appears in "America the Beautiful." Then you can be a *Jeopardy!* contestant, as this author once was.

**AUSPICIOUS** means that there are a lot of good omens indicating that something is going to turn out well. If you happen to see a large number of people wearing scarlet footwear in October, it is auspicious. It means the Red Sox are going to win the World Series. Yes!

**BEASTLY** means thoroughly unpleasant and has nothing to do with beasts, really, unless you are describing a warthog or a hyena, both of which are beastly as well as being beasts.

**BILIOUS** has several meanings, and one pretty disgusting one is "about to vomit." Another is "extremely unpleasant to look at," and that is what the Willoughby twins meant when they described their sweater as bilious.

**CONFECTIONARY** has to do with candies. You can also spell it with an *e: confectionery* (remember that, if you are ever on *Wheel of Fortune*). A confectioner is a guy who makes or sells candy. Willy Wonka was a confectioner.

**CONSPIRACY** is a plan to do something subversive. Three guys planning a camping trip . . . nah, that's just three guys planning a camping trip. But three guys planning to take a camping trip and rob a bank along the way . . . that's a conspiracy.

**CONTEMPLATING** means thinking about something very calmly and seriously. Sometimes you will hear the phrase "contemplating your navel," which of course means thinking very seriously about your bellybutton, and makes no sense at all, because what dolt would do that? There is a whole order of nuns, incidentally, called contemplative nuns. They spend all their time thinking very calmly and seriously, but not about their navels. Maybe nuns don't even *have* navels. There is no way to know.

**CRYPTIC** means seeming to have a hidden meaning. If your mother says, "Consider yourself grounded, mister!" it is not at all cryptic. But if she says in a certain voice, "We need to talk," she is being cryptic. And you are about to be grounded.

**DESPICABLE** means deserving of contempt. I began to describe something despicable, but it was too upsetting so I stopped. You can come up with your own example.

**DIABOLICAL** means extremely cruel or evil. The French word for it is *diabolique*. There is a French movie called *Diabolique* that I saw more than fifty years ago, and it is still the scariest movie I have ever seen.

**EXPOSTULATION** means a sound that expresses disagreement or disapproval. "Yuck!" is an expostulation. So is "Arrrggghh."

**FORTUITOUS** means a good thing happening just by chance. If you buy a winning lottery ticket, it is very fortuitous. (Also very unlikely.) A better example (but boring compared to the lottery) is if it begins to rain unexpectedly but you have *fortuitously* brought an umbrella.

**GLOSSARY** means an alphabetical list of terms and their meanings, usually at the end of a book. Hey! We are right smack in the middle of a glossary right now!

**GLUTINOUS** means just what it sounds like: sticky and disgusting. When my dog has to take a pill, I disguise the pill by putting it inside a glutinous wad of mozzarella cheese, and he gulps it right down.

**HEINOUS** means shockingly evil or wicked. Right up there with *nefarious* and *reprehensible*.

**IGNOMINIOUS** means shamefully weak and ineffective. Oliver Twist saying, "Please sir, might I have some more?" would be ignominious, except that he isn't shameful, just sort of pathetic. This book has ignominious illustrations. They are shamefully weak because the person who drew them is not an artist.

**INSIGNIFICANT** means very unimportant and having no power at all. One ant on the sidewalk is insignificant. A three-year-old could step on it and smoosh it, though it wouldn't be a very nice thing to do. An entire army of fire ants is very significant, and a three-year-old should definitely get out of the way.

**IRASCIBLE** means having outbursts of bad temper. I myself had a very irascible third-grade teacher and it made for a miserable year.

**LUGUBRIOUS** means very gloomy or mournful. Some funeral directors are lugubrious. They make a very sad face and say, "I'm so sorry for your loss," but secretly they are probably thinking about who is going to win the Super Bowl.

**MALEVOLENT** means wanting to harm others or having an evil influence. Even though if you glance quickly at the word, it may look like "male violent," this word has nothing to do with males. It is actually pronounced mah-LEV-oh-lent. Some females are very malevolent.

**MELANCHOLY** means sad. "Come to me, my melancholy baby; cuddle up and don't be blue" is the beginning of a romantic old song. Bad comedians used to tell a joke that went like this: "My girlfriend is very melancholy. She has a body like a melon and a face like a collie." But that has nothing to do with the meaning of the word and I'm sorry I brought it up.

**METICULOUS** means extremely precise and careful. Surgeons have to be meticulous. Some people think great cooks are meticulous, but they are wrong. Great cooks read a recipe, maybe, but then they ignore the instructions and add extra garlic if they feel like it. Surgeons can't do that.

**NEFARIOUS** means utterly, completely wicked. The character in *The Wizard of Oz* could have been called the Nefarious Witch of the West but authors like to use the same beginning consonant, often. Perhaps L. Frank Baum crossed out *nefarious* after *wicked* came to his mind. Thank goodness, because *Nefarious* would be a terrible name for a musical.

**OBFUSCATE** means to make something unclear. Lawyers have a way of obfuscating.

**OBLIVIOUS** means unaware of or paying no attention. If you press the mute button on your remote at the right time, you can be oblivious to the commercials. I know someone who turns off his hearing aid when he is with boring people and becomes oblivious. Obliviousness can be a good thing at times. Not always.

**OBSEQUIOUS** means overly eager to please. The kid who is always raising his hand in class and saying, "I know! I know!" is usually pretty obsequious and it's no wonder nobody can stand him. *Smarmy* is kind of a neat word that means obsequious.

**OBSTRUCTION** is something—or someone—that causes a blockage or a hindrance. Once, years ago, I had to call a plumber because there was an obstruction in my bathtub drain, and it turned out that my two-year-old had stuffed his toy snake down the pipe. Unrelated to plumbing, "obstruction of justice" is actually a crime, if you do it on purpose, and a lot of people seem to.

**ODIOUS,** surprisingly, has nothing to do with smell. It just means something hateful or disgusting. Of course, something that smells bad and is also disgusting—like a drunk guy barfing on the sidewalk—would be odious and odoriferous at the same time. But an adorable baby skunk would be odoriferous without being odious, and a person making racist remarks while wearing expensive aftershave would be odious without being odoriferous.

**PATHETIC** means so inadequate as to be laughable. Beethoven wrote a sonata for the piano called "Pathetique"—which means "pathetic" in French—but it is not at all inadequate. Go figure.

**REGRETTABLE** means unfortunate, or causing feelings of shame or embarrassment. We have all done regrettable things in our lives. It is best to forget about them.

**REPREHENSIBLE** means highly unacceptable. Really, really highly.

**SURREPTITIOUS** means operating in a sneaky, stealthy way. Spies are always surreptitious. So are children who peek at their Christmas presents before Christmas.

**TYCOON** means somebody who has amassed great wealth and power in business. Usually a tycoon is a man, for some reason. Maybe Oprah Winfrey is a tycooness.

**UNKEMPT** means untidy and messy. My dictionary says it can also mean disorderly, but I know that a person can be arrested for being "drunk and disorderly" and I don't think someone can be arrested for being unkempt. Also, I don't think there is a word *kempt*—so what is that "un" all about? Beats me.

**VILLAINOUS** means typical of an evil person. Very obnoxious. You could have guessed that, of course, since you already know the word *villain*. In old movies, villains almost always had mustaches. I don't know why.

**WINSOME** means charming and innocent. The victims of villains are usually winsome and often have curls and long eyelashes.

# BIBLIOGRAPHY

*(Books of the past that are heavy on piteous but appealing orphans, ill-tempered and stingy relatives, magnanimous benefactors, and transformations wrought by winsome children)*

## THE ADVENTURES OF HUCKLEBERRY FINN
*by Mark Twain, published 1884.*
Orphan Huckleberry Finn builds a raft with his friend Jim and they sail down the Mississippi River hoping to get away from civilization. They never do. Undaunted, Huck vows to try again.

## ANNE OF GREEN GABLES
*by Lucy Maude Montgomery, published 1908.*
Eleven-year-old orphan Anne Shirley arrives at the Prince Edward Island farm of Marilla Cuthbert, who thought she was getting a boy to help with the chores and is dismayed at the arrival of the redheaded, talkative girl. Life at Green Gables is filled with ups and downs as Anne makes her way in the world and transforms everyone she meets. Like most literary orphans, she is wise, worthy, and self-possessed.

# THE BOBBSEY TWINS AND BABY MAY
*by Laura Lee Hope, published 1924.*

The Bobbsey family has two sets of twins who have many adventures and sometimes solve mysteries. In this book they find an abandoned baby on their doorstep. (The baby's nurse, it turns out, had been hit on the head with a can of soup and had forgotten where she left the baby.) The Bobbsey parents are considerably more welcoming than Mrs. Willoughby.

# A CHRISTMAS CAROL
*by Charles Dickens, published 1843.*

A miserly, misanthropic gentleman named Mr. Scrooge is haunted by his own sad past. Getting a glimpse of what the future might be like, he is able to change and become once again the kind-hearted, generous person he had once been. A boy named Tim is not an orphan but behaves like one.

# HEIDI
*by Johanna Spyri, published 1872.*

Little Heidi, orphaned as an infant, is taken at age five by her selfish aunt to live with her ill-tempered recluse of a grandfather high up in the Swiss Alps. Her friends there include the illiterate goat-herd, Peter. Later she convinces a crippled girl named Clara to get out of her wheelchair and walk.

## JAMES AND THE GIANT PEACH
*by Roald Dahl, published 1961.*
Orphaned by a zoo mishap when he is eight, James must live with two evil aunts, Spiker and Sponge. Some magical elements intervene, involving over-large fruit, and the wretched aunts are mashed and destroyed, while James goes on to find happiness.

## JANE EYRE
*by Charlotte Bronte, published 1847.*
The penniless orphan Jane Eyre grows up and secures a position at Thornfield Hall, acting as governess to the spoiled niece of her employer, Mr. Rochester. After many mysteries and near disasters, Jane and her employer fall in love, marry, and presumably live happily ever after.

# LITTLE WOMEN

*by Louisa May Alcott, published 1868.*

Sisters Meg, Jo, Beth, and Amy live with their mother, whom they call Marmee, while their father is off in the Civil War. They have many adventures and some misfortunes. Meg is mature and sensible. Jo is literary and boyish. Amy is vain and foolish. Beth is saintly and dies.

# MARY POPPINS

*by P. L. Travers, published 1934.*

Mary Poppins is not at all like the cheerful, spritely movie person played by Julie Andrews. She is a stern, cross, vain, and mysterious nanny who arrives on the wind at the home of the Banks family in London to care for their four children, who are not orphans. Ms. Poppins does not sing, ever, and would not like being portrayed as someone who did.

# POLLYANNA

*by Eleanor H. Porter, published 1913.*

An orphaned child named Pollyanna goes east by train to live with her ill-tempered Aunt Polly. She finds ways to be glad about everything, even orphanhood, poverty, and a broken leg; and she changes everyone, including Aunt Polly, with her cheerful disposition.

## RAGGED DICK

*by Horatio Alger Jr., published 1867.*
An orphaned young boy with bad clothing struggles to escape poverty. Hard work, honesty, and a wealthy benefactor who sees his worth make things come out well for the boy.

## THE SECRET GARDEN

*by Frances Hodgson Burnett, published 1909.*
Newly orphaned Mary Lennox is sent to live with her uncle, Archibald Craven, at Misselthwaite Manor. He doesn't seem to like her much. But she makes an environmentally conscious friend named Dickon, and meets a sickly boy named Colin, whom she persuades to get out of his wheelchair and walk. Together the three children take up gardening and thrive.

## Toby Tyler; or, Ten Weeks with the Circus

*by James Otis, published 1923.*

An orphan named Toby runs away and joins the circus, but it is not a happy experience. His employer is a villain named Mr. Lord. The only one who loves him is a monkey. But the monkey dies.

Don't miss out on the Willoughby family's continued adventures in their sanctimonious sequel!

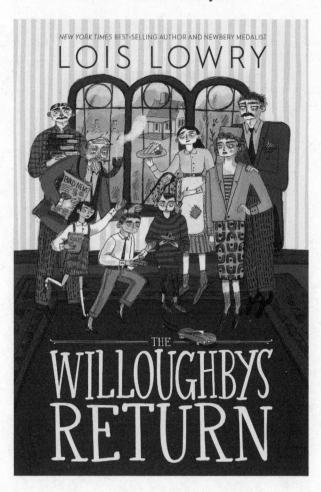

NEW YORK TIMES BEST-SELLING AUTHOR AND NEWBERY MEDALIST

# LOIS LOWRY

THE

# WILLOUGHBYS RETURN

# 1

The front page of the *New York Times,* on a Thursday in June:

## CONGRESS VOTES OVERWHELMINGLY TO BAN CANDY, CITES DENTAL HEALTH

On the same day, on an inside page of a Zurich newspaper:

## AMERICAN COUPLE, FROZEN IN SWISS MOUNTAINS FOR THREE DECADES, THAW SPONTANEOUSLY, APPEAR UNHARMED

These two events, it was later proved, were related. It's complicated.[1]

---

[1] So pay attention. It will be confusing at first. But it's worth hanging in there. And there won't be a quiz.

# 2

High on a mountain in Switzerland (one of the Alps, though a minor Alp, not a particularly well-known Alp, not the Matterhorn or one of those postcard-y ones), an odd, lumpy, ice-encrusted shape began to move slightly, causing the glistening snow to shift.

It had been very warm and sunny for days. Weeks, actually—even months. Across the globe, glaciers had shrunk and icebergs had dissolved. Now, on this insignificant Alp, which had been snow-covered for eons, suddenly rocks began to appear, sleek with water from the snowmelt. Here and there a green stem emerged, and an occasional flower.

And now, a moving lump.

Then, beside the first strangely moving shape, another large, snowy lump shifted. Amazingly, from one of the shifting mounds, a hand emerged. It brushed some snow aside, revealing an entire arm. Then a second arm appeared.

The first mound sat up, and the two arms, moist

from the melted snow, began to brush snow and wipe water from a face. It was a newly defrosted face, male, with a glowering frown. It looked around, perceived the second mound nearby, and reached over to give it a poke. Then another poke, and another. Finally the second lump sat up, also frowning. This one appeared to be female (though it is hard to tell, with a lump).

"I bet anything my hair is an absolute mess," the second lump grumbled.

But the first lump paid no attention. He was testing his stiff fingers, tapping at them to dislodge a few ice particles. Finally he reached down to his right hip and removed a soggy wallet from his pocket.

"I knew it!" he groaned, prying open the wet leather. "My money is ruined! Sodden. Practically *dissolved*. And all stuck together in a messy wad."

"Our dollars?"

"No, those ridiculous Swiss francs[2] they made us get. Clearly inferior. American dollars wouldn't deteriorate like this."

"Well, are they usable enough for food, at least? I'm hungry."

[2] Most countries in Europe started using Euros in 1995. But not Switzerland. They still like their francs.

"Of course they'll take our money. They're all crooks here."

The woman (because they were a pair: man and woman) groaned, struggled to her feet, then knelt. "Where's my purse? I don't see my purse." On her hands and knees, she began pawing through the wet snow. "Here!" she said. "Here it is! But yuck—it's drenched!"

"Don't worry about it. And stand up! You look like a cockroach, crawling around that way. Come on. We'll make our way down to the village and get a quick lunch—not that they have any decent food in this godforsaken place. Then we'll get the first train out." The man stood upright with some difficulty and replaced the wet billfold in his hip pocket.

Finally the pair, grumbling and complaining, managed to stumble slowly down the side of the thawing Alp, passing on the low slopes meadows dotted with cows, toward the tiny village at its foot. The one main street was lined with brightly painted homes and dotted with flower boxes filled with petunias and geraniums. They found a table at a small café, where they ate heartily of a veal stew and each had three glasses of quite a good wine. But they were thwarted when the bill was brought to their table.

"I'm so sorry," the waiter said as he looked with dismay at the sodden mass of Swiss francs that the man offered him. "Ve can't accept vet money. But—"

"*Vet?* Good lord, man—can't you even say the word *wet?*"

"Apologies, sir. I vill try harder. Damp vould be okay, perhaps. But soggy vet is bad."

"Give them a credit card, dear," the woman suggested.

With a loud sigh the man pried a platinum card loose from his waterlogged wallet.

"I'm sorry, Mr. . . ." The waiter looked carefully at the card. "Ah, Mr. Villoughby. But this credit card expired many years ago."

"It's WILLOUGHBY, you idiot! Why can't you dolts pronounce a *W* the way normal people do?"

"I'm wery sorry, sir. I vish I could," the waiter replied, with a roll of his eyes that implied he did not vish any such thing.

The maître d' appeared, smiling politely. "Is there a problem?" he asked. Then he looked more closely at the ill-tempered couple. "Oh. I see you've defrosted. You're still damp."

"*Defrosted?*" bellowed Mr. Willoughby. "What on earth—"

"You were frozen," the maître d' explained, and peered at the date on the credit card. "And now you've thawed. It's happened to a number of climbers."

"And many goats, as vell," the waiter added. "It's the varming."

"The *vat?* I mean: *what?*"

"Global varming, sir."

Mrs. Willoughby sighed. "You never believed in that, Henry. But *now* look." She patted her own head. "My hairstyle is hopelessly out of date. Take me home, right away."

"Bring me a telephone," Mr. Willoughby demanded.

"Of course," the maître d' said. He nodded to the waiter, who scurried away to find a phone. "You must call your family."

"Family?" Henry Willoughby said, looking startled.

His wife groaned. "Oh lord, we have those horrible children. Do we know their phone number, Henry? Do we even know where they live?"

Her husband shrugged. "I forget. But we don't have to worry about them. We hired that nanny, remember?"

"Oh, yes. The nanny."

"Anyway, it doesn't matter about them," her husband muttered. "I'm calling my bank."

The maître d' smiled politely. "You should certainly do that," he said. "You owe us vun hundred and twelve Swiss francs for your dinner. I do hope you enjoyed the weal? And may I pour you some more of this vine?"

# 3

Sad to say, the nanny had passed away some years before. She was immortalized now in an oil portrait that
hung in—

Oh, wait. A little history is necessary here. A little
filling in of the details.

Many years before—thirty years to be exact—Mr.
and Mrs. Willoughby had embarked on an extended
vacation,[3] leaving their four children behind. They
didn't like the children very much (and to be honest,
the children didn't like them, either), and so it was not
a tragedy for them to be separated. But it would have
been illegal for them to leave the children all alone
(the eldest, Tim, was just twelve). To keep things on
the up-and-up, Mr. Willoughby had advertised for a
nanny and had hired the no-nonsense woman, who ap-

---

[3] They used the Reprehensible Travel Agency. The company
ceased operation some years ago after consistently bad re-
views on Yelp.

peared at the front door on her first day of work with a starched and folded apron in her satchel.

Then, when their parents did not return (because they had stupidly worn shorts and sandals to go mountain climbing) and finally the Swiss government had announced that the couple had frozen solid on an Alp, perched on an icy ledge from which they could not be retrieved (though for a few coins they could be viewed by telescope from several tourist locations), and the house in which they had lived was sold, the children and Nanny had to rethink their living arrangements. Fortunately, Nanny was very enterprising. She took a job in the nearby home (mansion, actually) of a man, founder and president of Consolidated Confectionaries, Inc., who had made a fortune manufacturing candy. All four children, and even their cat, went with her.

And guess what! The billionaire, Commander Melanoff, fell in love with her! Well, why wouldn't he? She was a wonderful cook, a fine housekeeper, a no-nonsense woman, and a dutiful caretaker not only of the children but of Commander Melanoff himself. She trimmed his mustache and sprinkled cinnamon on his oatmeal. He was a very rich and very lonely bachelor. In time there was a wedding and a happily-ever-after.

Except—

Oh dear. Eventually, after many years, she passed away. And now she was an oil portrait hanging on the front wall of the mansion. Commander Melanoff had commissioned the portrait from a famous painter, and he had directed that the portrait show Nanny the way he fondly remembered her: with her no-nonsense expression, and oven mitts on her hands. He had installed special lighting so that she seemed to glow.

The commander, an elderly man now, lived in a palatial suite of rooms on the third floor. He spent his time reading history and composing poetry.[4] All of his poems were about Nanny. Whenever he was on the first floor, he stood in front of the portrait, gazing at it and reciting his odes to her memory.

Sometimes his grandson, eleven-year-old Richie, covered his ears and begged, "Not that one, Grandpa!" when the commander began to intone with reverence: *"There once was a woman named Nanny . . ."*

"That's inappropriate, Grandpa!" Richie said, be-

---

[4] So far he had composed seven sonnets, twenty-two haiku, and a nineteen-line villanelle. His favorite, though, was a limerick that was slightly naughty.

cause he knew the next line, which referred to Nanny's backside and began *"Who had an incomparable . . ."*

"Nothing is inappropriate if it is true," the commander replied, and continued his recitation. But Richie chanted *"La la la"* very loudly and ran off down the hall so that he couldn't hear the poem.

Oh, wait. We have to explain Richie. The Willoughby children had all grown up, of course. They had gone to college and taken jobs and moved away to live their various lives. All but Tim. Tim, the eldest, had always been a clever boy. Now forty-two years old, with the blessing of Commander Melanoff, he had taken over the candy manufacturing company, which had continued its enormous and profitable success. He and his wife lived in the mansion with their little boy. Richie was Tim Willoughby's son.

"What's wrong?" Richie asked, entering the large dining room where his parents were having breakfast. "I can hear Grandpa sort of *yowling* up on the third floor."

Then he looked at his father, who had just crumpled the *New York Times*, thrown it onto the floor, and was pounding the mahogany table with his fist. At the edge of his placemat, his coffee cup had overturned and a dark puddle of coffee was expanding.

At the other end of the table, Richie's mother rang the small silver bell that summoned the maid, who appeared instantly through an unobtrusive door.

"Clean that up, please, before it damages the rug," Ruth Willoughby directed the maid, indicating the spilled coffee with a nod of her head.

"And the paper, ma'am? Shall I smooth it out?" the maid asked, indicating the crumpled *New York Times* on the carpet. But Richie's mother murmured, "No, get rid of it." So the maid wiped up the spilled coffee, then collected the ruined newspaper and took it to the kitchen to add to the recyclables. (The Willoughby family, and Commander Melanoff as well, were all very environmentally aware.)

Because the *New York Times* had now disappeared, Tim Willoughby would not have an opportunity to read the small article about the amazing reappearance of the frozen couple in Switzerland.

Too bad. He would have been very interested in that article, because the newly thawed Americans were his parents.

But he had been distracted by the major headline and front-page news from the US Congress. The banning of candy! How could this have happened? Well, he knew exactly how it had happened! It was the dentists! The American Dental Association! They had been lobbying for months against candy. They ran ads on TV showing openmouthed children displaying rotting, discolored teeth while the voice of a mournful dentist explained gloomily how if only they had not eaten candy, they would not have reached this sad state.

And finally all of the senators and representatives had been convinced. Well, not *all*. An elderly Democratic senator from Vermont, a bald man with ill-fitting false teeth and a liking for gummy bears, had voted against the bill. And there were two Republicans who had found it amusing to show up on the floor of the House of Representatives sucking on lollipops. They had also voted no.

But they were the only ones. And now, with the candy-ban bill voted into law, the newspaper said, candy was to be immediately removed from stores across the country. Factories would be closed down. Halloween trick-or-treating would be reworked—maybe comic books could become the new treats?

Richie was still standing in the doorway when his grandfather, wearing a bathrobe, came down the long stairway. He was no longer yowling, but he was snuffling and dabbing at his eyes. At the foot of the stairs he turned, as he always did, and bowed his head in front of Nanny's portrait. Richie cringed, hoping his grandpa would not begin to recite a naughty poem. But Commander Melanoff only murmured, "Nanny, Nanny, Nanny . . ."

Then he turned, patted Richie briefly on the head, and entered the dining room. "You've heard?" he asked Tim.

"Yes," Richie's father replied in a low voice.

"We're ruined, aren't we?"

Tim Willoughby nodded. "Ruined. Totally."

In the silence that followed, Richie asked, "Is it okay if I go out and play?"

His father stared at him. "What do you plan to play with?"

Richie thought. "Um, my Firepulse Innovation top-grain leather basketball."

"Is that new?" his father asked.

"Yes. I ordered it last week and it just came yesterday. I'm not sure if I like it yet. I might get a Spalding TF-1000."

Richie had always been allowed to order whatever toys or gadgets he wanted. Billionaires (and their children, and even their grandchildren) can do that, of course.

His father rose from his seat, went to his son, and put his arm around him. "Richie, we're going to have to cut back."

"Huh?"

"You go ahead outside to play with your basketball. But don't order anything else. We're destitute. We've been destroyed."

"Destroyed?"

"Yes. By dentists."